TRUE
CHAMPIONS

TRUE Champions

THE GOOD GUYS IN AMERICAN SPORTS SPEAK OUT

Compiled By

M I K E T O W L E

THE SUMMIT GROUP
FORT WORTH, TEXAS

Published by The Summit Group
1227 West Magnolia • Fort Worth, Texas 76104

Copyright © 1994 by The Summit Group

Library Of Congress Cataloging-in-Publication Data

True champions: the good guys in American sports speak out/ compiled by Mike
  Towle.
     p.cm.
     ISBN 1-56530-126-9: $22.95
     1. Athletes—United States—Biography. 2. Sports—United States—
Religious aspects—Christianity. 3. Social values. I. Towle, Mike.
GV697.A1T78 1994
796'.092'2—dc20
  [B}   94-8917
                                                                     CIP

To Andy

TABLE OF CONTENTS

Contents

FOREWORD

There's no question that there is an incredible responsibility that goes with being a professional athlete, serving as a role model in our society. But at the same time, I don't feel any extra pressure with that, because I don't believe I have any more responsibility than anybody else in this role does. I just accept that role and do the best I can representing what I believe to be right and good. Every parent—in fact, everyone in a position to be seen by others—has that incredible responsibility to be the light of God. How else are people going to know who God is? If I'm faithful to what I know, then it will show.

It's scary as to what is going on in our society today. You can see the deterioration of the United States in the morals of the people, and even in the laws that are being made. The pervasive thinking in this day and age is what makes life as a society kind of frightening. Things such as behavior and attitudes that are becoming acceptable shouldn't necessarily be so. Furthermore, you can't really argue with people if they don't believe in God, because it doesn't make any difference to them when you try to tell them it's not okay with God to do certain things. It's not a matter of arguing. You see what's going on and all you can really do is set the right example.

The word of God is like a lion in a cage. Don't spend your time defending it; just let the lion out of the cage. Let the words you speak be strong and let the power of righteousness come forth. That's how I use it—I don't debate with people about my beliefs and about what I think is good or bad, even when they say they don't believe in God. All I know is that what He says is the truth. I don't have to defend it.

With anybody who is a real man or woman of God—as I'm sure is the case with most or all of the people in *True Champions*—is that there is a struggle there; there is a compassion there; and there is a mutual love there that surpasses anything most people can understand. It's a kinship. When I see a real heart for God, I have a real love for that person. True men and women of God feel that same thing. It doesn't mean I talk to other Christian athletes every day or am the best of friends with all of them, but I do appreciate who and what they stand for, and respect that in them. So it's a tremendous boost to me when I see other athletes like that. If I get a chance to encourage others, it's a real blessing.

Walking the walk is always difficult, no question about it. It starts right in my own home in terms of being the best husband and father I can be. It's a battle sometimes, because the devil can come between you and your wife in a thousand different ways. Yet, while life is a struggle for many of us, we can't use a bunch of excuses. We all face our own challenges and we need to remain faithful to what we know is right.

The one thing I tell kids a lot is that, "You don't have to do things just because you see it all the time—because other people do it." That's not a great reason to do anything. One day you have to answer to the Lord—why you did what you did and why you lived your life the way you did. Saying you did something because those other people did it is not a good enough reason. In that respect, you have to decide for yourself what's important. For example, before I got married, I could see that there weren't a lot of great marriages out there. But that didn't mean I had to expect or accept that in my own life. Anything I have learned so far about being a good husband and father has come from the good Lord. The encouragement I would give kids is that there is a better life and you don't have to live a defeated life.

I actually take a little bit of joy in being different in the sense that I try to live my life as a good, righteous person. We're supposed to be different, but not in an oddball, goofball kind of way. We're supposed to be different in a positive way. Although people see me as different—even my teammates—they respect me very much for where I stand. I come out and compete night in and night out, and teammates respect me for what I do on the floor. They also respect me as a man, because they know if I give them my word, I will stand by it. Yeah, maybe it's different, but it's not a negative different. They don't say, "Well, he's a goofball; he doesn't live like the rest of us, he can't relate to any of us." That just isn't true. I've been where all of them have been and I don't try to act like I haven't. I think they respect that in me.

—*David Robinson*
National Basketball Association All-Star
San Antonio Spurs

PREFACE

Preface

Through more than twenty years of covering sports events and sporting people for various publications ranging from small-town newspapers to national publications, I have had both the pleasure and the burden of dealing with athletes, coaches, managers, general managers, owners, and agents of all kinds.

Regardless of the story being covered or written, sports journalism, like most anything else, boils down to a people business. We know who we like and who we don't like; and we in the media know the "good guys" from the "others." Of course, this is a two-way street, and I can only hope that most sports people I have ever dealt with have had a favorable perception of me, if any perception at all. Yes, there are two types of people in the world: those who want to be liked and those who won't admit it. I fall into the former category.

Let me fast forward by saying that this is a book I have truly enjoyed putting together, although the grind-it-out stuff such as deadlines, rejections for inclusion in the book, and late nights and weekends lost to putting this book together have added a few gray hairs. But it has been worthwhile. This book allowed me to write about the good guys in sports, in their own words and with a transparency to their hearts and minds.

My first duty in making a book out of all this was to put together a "wish list" of athletes and coaches that I knew to be "good guys," with strong Christian values. Every project of such magnitude needs some sort of focus—a game plan, if you will—and that is the way I chose. Why? I believe people anchored in Christian values are not only good people when putting their game faces on in public, but also have made commitments to be good people in their personal and family lives. This doesn't mean the people included in this book are any "better" than those from other slices of life. It means only that they are willing to admit their faults while accepting the responsibility that goes with being a positive public role model.

Putting this book together over a three-month whirlwind of activity would not have been possible without dozens of people lending me their support. At times, it frighteningly looked like I would never round up enough of the sports figures needed to fill out this book. But through the efforts of many behind-the-front-lines people and an accommodating spirit by the twenty-five athletes and coaches, this book came together on schedule. For that, I will be forever grateful to the following people:

First, to my wife and best friend, Holley. She has been as excited about this project as I have, and has been a guiding light and buffer for me during the trying times balancing this book with my other career demands. Patience is a virtue, and Holley has plenty of that.

To my Summit Group colleagues, especially Mark Hulme, Len Oszustowicz, David Gavin, Brent Lockhart, Joe Bishop, Daniel Collins, Troy Reese, Sean Walker, David Sims, Cheryl Corbitt, and Kevin Fletcher; I thank them not only for their willingness to make this book a part of our company's list, but for their counsel and support during the course of putting this book together.

To Louie Hulme, my esteemed copy editor, and Tesa Riddle, my proofer. Their attention to detail always is a big help.

To Ty Benz, Texas Christian University senior, budding sports writer, and Summit Group editorial intern. Ty hit the ground running when he came to work for me, diligently putting together the biographical information and acquiring all the photos needed to make this a real book.

To Dianna Archey and Wendy Wright, transcribing typists. They put in a lot of time on flexible hours to see this through.

To Sandy Lichtenberger, The Summit Group office manager. Sandy and her assistants, Kim Symons and Taryn Wheat, were invaluable in juggling hundreds of telephone messages, faxes, and express mail related to this book.

Chapter   One

LARRY MIZE

M A S T E R S   G O L F   C H A M P I O N

speaks out on…

SELF-ESTEEM/SIGNIFICANCE:

The biggest thing to me with self-esteem is realizing the only reason that I'm significant is because of what Christ did for me and what God did for all of us. Through Jesus Christ coming into this world, walking through terrible agony and suffering, dying a horrible death, and rising from the dead, we all get the chance to experience significance.

In everything we do, it is so easy to get caught up in the idea that you are what you are through what you do for a living or something else along that line. For me, as a golfer, it's real easy to get caught up in the line of thinking, when you might say, "Hey, I'm important because I've won this particular tournament, or because I'm a golfer on the PGA (Professional Golfers' Association) Tour. That's where my self-esteem and personal feeling of significance comes from." No, my significance comes from the fact that God loves me and He loves us all enough to have sent Jesus to die for us.

He paid the price for our sins. That's something that has been important to me. I think back to when I won the Masters (in 1987). I got caught up in that a little bit, the idea of being a Masters champion. That went to my head a little bit, although I was soon humbled after that. I'm very thankful that I was humbled, because it forced me again to remember why I was significant and that whatever I do on the golf course is fine and great, but it still doesn't change the fact that my significance comes only through Jesus Christ.

When I talk about humility, it means realizing that without Christ I'm nothing. I have to thank Him for everything. You know, that just keeps things in perspective. Unfortunately, I don't keep things in their right perspective 100 percent of the time, but I work hard to keep them there. I know I'm no better than anyone else and that I'm lost without Jesus Christ. That's what I'm talking about with humility.

It was really not until about May of 1989, two years after winning the Masters, that I realized I had fallen off track. I hadn't won a tournament since the 1987 Masters and had lost sight of who I really was and why I was out there on the golf course. I called up Larry Moody, who leads us out here with the PGA Tour Bible study. Larry straightened me out, letting me know that I was to the point where I was making myself miserable. It had gotten to where I was thinking about not playing golf anymore. Now that's pretty crazy.

Larry reminded me that he felt God wanted me to be playing golf, and that my significance came from Christ and not from the victory on the golf course. Sure, it was okay to enjoy the win and everything else that goes with it. But it was much more important to win to glorify Christ while remembering what He did for all of us through His love.

I definitely shed a few tears that day, getting rid of some of the baggage I had been carrying around. I started remembering why I am significant, realizing that what I needed to do was go out there on the golf course, be myself, and not try to be some Masters champion or someone else that I'm not. It was really a great experience, because I think God uses times like that to mature us. It was definitely a maturing time, as hard as it was on me. You don't enjoy going through times of hardship like that, but as Paul says in the New Testament, "Rejoice in everything, even the bad times." I rejoice now, looking back and realizing all the good things that came about because of the hard times that I have been through. It's just a maturing process—a blessing in disguise.

It's funny, at least for me in the game of golf; you work hard to try to be the best you can be, and then you win a big tournament like the Masters and suddenly you quit doing the things that got you there. You start trying to do new things, maybe different things with your swing, to become even better. That's not right. As far as golf goes, when you win a major, you've reached a pinnacle. That's when you need to realize, Hey, I need to keep doing what I have been doing. I don't need to push myself harder and beat my head against the wall trying to do something that I'm not.

If you win the Masters or one of the other three majors, it doesn't get any better as far as golf goes. Keep going with what got you there. Don't try to live up to something or get your expectations so high that you're just going to be frustrated. And that's what I did. I learned from it, and it has paid off since then.

What happened to me was that I wasn't living up to the heightened expectations of suddenly being the Masters champion. I had things all out of perspective. Everybody wants to win, and I want to win, but the main thing I want to do is reach my potential and play as well as I can. That's all you can do. But back then, I was trying to force things and make things happen. It took me a while and some hard trials before I understood that I was trying to control things that were beyond my control. It was all very frustrating. The only thing frustration can do for you is get you to the point where you just get fed up with it all, and say, "If I can't do any better than this, I should go do something else." I kind of sit back and laugh about it now, because it was pretty immature and silly on my part. But then again, it's part of the learning process and part of maturity, and that's why I'm very thankful I went through all that.

It's still a struggle, and I think I'm correct in saying it's always going to be a struggle. It's never going to be easy. These days, I do a

> **Don't try to live up to something or get your expectations so high that you're just going to be frustrated.**

better job of struggling with keeping things in perspective. As long as I'm making progress and feeling good about it, I'm happy with where I am in my walk. We live in an imperfect world, and bad things happen. We don't have the answers for everything, but we do have the answer that we have a loving, good God and He is in control. Life isn't always going to work out like we want it to. But if we have faith and trust in Him, it's all going to work out.

Through His spirit, He gives me the peace and the joy that I didn't have before I accepted Him. People talk about that, saying, "I don't want to wait until I die to find out if I'm going to heaven to be with Christ." My answer to that is kind of like what it says in John 10:10 about Him coming to die for us so that we might have life more abundantly. I have a peace and a joy that I never had before accepting Christ. So I look forward to meeting God, and living and being in heaven with Him. I also have a much fuller and better life here, so I just continue to work hard to keep things in perspective and work hard on what I can control.

I need to work hard to do everything I can do, because otherwise I'm cheating me and I'm not doing the best job I can for God. A lot of times people ask me what I think about on the golf course. One of my thoughts I've been keeping in my head is, Who am I trying to please out there? Am I trying to please the spectators? Am I trying to please friends back home? You know, I'd love to please everybody, but I need to stay focused on God. If I do that, everything will be okay. My job is to love God and keep His commandments, and please Him. That's what I think about.

That kind of spiritual commitment enabled me to have a really good year on the golf course in 1993. My faith in God is right in the middle of everything. It's the most important thing to me, with my family being next, and then golf. It is a struggle, but it's fun and I enjoy doing it for Christ. It's gratifying. If I wasn't doing it for Him, I wouldn't have the gratification that I get out of it.

Starting off in the early part of the 1994 season, I was kind of having some of the same struggles I had after the Masters win. But I see it more clearly now. I see my tendencies and I can work on them. My previous struggles helped shape the good year I had in 1993. They made me realize I couldn't go out and put a stranglehold on the golf course or the game. You know you have to go out there and let things happen. Enjoy it and have a good time, and then get out of your own way. Golf is not a game where you can just grab something by the throat and do it. At least, it isn't for me. You've got to go out there and let things happen.

Coming off one of my best years last year (1993), I had to be careful not to get in my own way, pressing and trying and worrying about things I can't control. I love to win golf tournaments, and I'm competitive to a fault. But my main goal out there is to please God and glorify Him in what I do. That's the great thing about the tough times; they're actually great learning times.

One of the times when I really felt strong in my walk as a believer playing golf was at Tucson (for the Northern Telecom Open) last year. It was a Sunday. Keep in mind I still hadn't won another event on the PGA Tour since winning at Augusta in 1987. Well, as it turned out that Sunday in Tucson, I won. But what was even more important to me was that I was having a great time. I was just letting things happen. Again, I knew that God was in control. Really, winning wasn't the most important thing that day, even though there have been times in my life when winning was the most important thing. That's when I get myself in trouble. However, I just felt really at peace in Tucson. Sure, I was nervous coming down the stretch, no doubt about it. But I really felt good about it, and it was a neat time, because I wasn't getting caught up in things that make me worry or which I can't control. That feeling I had on the golf course is hard to explain. It was really a peaceful and comforting feeling. It was a special week.

Sure, I was nervous coming down the stretch, no doubt about it. But I really felt good about it, and it was a neat time, because I wasn't getting caught up in things that make me worry or which I can't control.

Then later in the year, there was that week in December of playing in the Johnny Walker World Championship. I think that was another week where I really had things in perspective. Obviously, I was playing really well; I was putting really well, and my concentration was great. But after Saturday's round, I was nervous being in the lead. I was nervous that night and woke up Sunday morning still feeling nervous, perhaps a little more nervous than I expected to be. I then got to thinking, You know, I'm flying home Sunday night, and on Monday we're going to go to Augusta to see my parents for an early Christmas. Then we would return home Christmas Eve, and get ready for Santa and to celebrate Christ's birthday.

The neat thing was teeing off that Sunday. I told myself, Larry, go out there; just let it go and do your best; and remember one thing— no matter what happens—you're fixing to have a great Christmas with your family. Bonnie and I had just had our third son. So it was going to be his first Christmas. It dawned on me that the tournament wasn't the most important thing to me. Having a great time with my family was what it's really all about. Keeping everything in perspective that way allowed me to go out there, let it go, and play up to my potential.

That Sunday round, under the heat of competitive pressure, probably was my best ever. Shooting a 65 in circumstances like that was something I won't soon forget. At other times, I've put too much emphasis on a tournament and too much heat on myself. It's tough to play golf like that. Everybody's makeup is different, but for me, that's the way I see it. I was very pleased with myself because I concentrated and worked hard to play the best I could. I had some peace teeing off that day.

SPORTSMANSHIP:

Fair play is one of the great things about golf. It's called a gentleman's game and there is a code of ethics. You can try to cheat out there, but then you haven't accomplished anything. If you bend the rules or whatever, whether anybody knows it or not, you know it and know you've accomplished nothing. That's the great thing about golf—trying to see what you can accomplish and what you can master that day or that week or that year in your career. There's such a satisfaction in doing it right and not breaking the rules. That's the way golf is supposed to be played.

When the ball moves and they call a penalty on you, you hate it. At the same time, you really feel good that you've done the right thing. It's all going to come out in the wash. If you don't do the right thing, it's going to come back and get you sooner or later in some other fashion. Golf is a great game, and doing it by the rules is fun. I take my hat off to guys who call penalty strokes on themselves, knowing that no one else saw them and that they probably could have gotten away with it.

Oftentimes, people ask me, "What about the idea of sportsmanship when you go up against another player?" Or, "What happens when you go head to head against a good Christian friend of yours; is there a problem?" I say, "Shoot, no. I want to beat him; he wants to beat me." There's nothing wrong with that. That's just good, clean competition and sportsmanship. I want the guys I play against to play well. I wish them the best, because if I play up to my potential and play well, then I'm pleased. It's still disappointing when you lose, but you have the satisfaction of knowing that you played well and did everything you could.

You want the guys to play well so that you beat them when they play well. It's a lot more fun when you do that than when someone plays poorly and you sneak in a win. And in golf, I'm competing against the golf course, anyway. If you get too tied in with gamesmanship with another player, you're going to get in trouble. A lot of times, the one you have to beat is yourself. Get out of your way, and enable yourself to concentrate. Cheating is not going to get you anywhere, whether it's golf or anything else in life. Cheating is a killer. It ruins everything for which you've worked. That's the great thing about golf. You're on your own. You get to call your shots, and it's a great game.

❈

LARRY MIZE

Professional golfer Larry Mize will always be remembered as the person who made "the impossible shot" that won the 1987 Masters Championship. On the second hole of a sudden-death playoff, Mize holed a 140-foot chip shot at Augusta's eleventh hole to beat Greg Norman. (Seve Ballesteros, also tied for the lead after seventy-two holes of regulation, was eliminated on the first playoff hole.)

With Norman's ball lying on the green in two, Mize's ball was well to the right of the green, almost fifty yards away from the hole. The cup was on the far left side of the green, not far from the pond bordering the left edge of the putting surface. Using a sand wedge, Mize holed out the chip for a birdie, and won the tournament after Norman missed his long birdie putt.

The Masters victory thrust Mize into golf's spotlight. By year's end, he had amassed $561,407 in PGA Tour winnings, placing him among that year's top-ten money winners.

Mize's list of accomplishments has grown since the Masters triumph. In 1987, he represented the United States in Ryder Cup competition. In 1990, he finished second in three tournaments and won more than $660,000 in prize money.

He had his best year yet in 1993, winning the Northern Telecom Open and the Buick Open on tour. He then closed out the year with a ten-shot victory over Fred Couples in the Johnny Walker World Championship. During the 1993 Tour season, Mize posted seven top-ten finishes and pocketed a career-high $724,000.

Going into the 1994 season, Mize stood less than $100,000 away from becoming one of the select few to top the $4 million mark in career PGA Tour earnings.

Mize and his wife Bonnie have three sons; David, Patrick, and Robert.

LARRY MIZE'S FIVE TIPS ON LIFE AND GOLF:

1. Before I got married, a friend of mine told me that I would get out of marriage exactly what I put into it. I get back so much more than I deserve.

2. I want to be *a* winner, not necessarily *the* winner. I want to be a winner for Jesus Christ, keep His commandments, and do the right thing. A lot of times, you end up being a winner both ways. Doing what the Bible says and glorifying Christ are things I want to do and are things I think about on the golf course.

3. In golf, check your alignment. If you aren't lined up properly, you won't hit the ball where you want it to go. After a while, bad alignment will cause bad swings as you try to compensate. You should lay your clubs down at your feet at least once a week to check where you are really aimed.
4. Practice your short game at least 50 percent of the time you are practicing. You will play better and get into your buddy's pocket more often.
5. Practice trouble shots so that you will know what to do when you get into those situations during an actual round.

Author's royalties donated to Search Ministries

Chapter   Two

BRETT BUTLER

A L L - S T A R   B A S E B A L L   P L A Y E R

speaks out on…

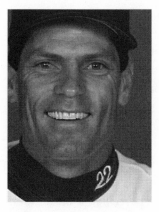

MEETING THE CHALLENGE:

My character is such that when it comes to pressure, I have usually been able to make a positive out of a negative. I wanted to be a major-league baseball player as far back as I can remember, even knowing that I have probably always been the smallest guy on whatever team I've played on.

When I was in high school, my coach said, "You'll never make it; you can't even play on our team." Later, he said, "What makes you think you can go play at Arizona State?" In fact, we were at our post-season team banquet, and after the coach handed me my varsity letter and I told him I was going to go play at Arizona State, he said, "Well, Brett Butler thinks he's going to go play at Arizona State, which is the best baseball school in the nation, when he couldn't even play for us." As time went on, I was able to use those words as an incentive to do better.

Later, after I had made it to the big leagues, my high school coach asked me what he had done wrong to overlook me in high school. I said, "You never gave me a chance to play, but I thank you for that because you were kind of a driving force behind my wanting to prove you wrong." With me, it has always been other people's negative attitude of "He'll never do it," or "He is too little," or "He can't do this; he can't do that," that I have always tried to use to my advantage in trying to succeed.

My best friend growing up was my father, Jerry. One of his comments to me was, "Son, if you don't believe in yourself, nobody else will." Keeping that in mind has been helpful in handling pressure—in meeting many of the challenges that have been set out before me. If I didn't believe I could do it, then surely nobody else was going to believe I could. In a nutshell, that's what handling pressure—not only in baseball, but with everything in life, such as with my family—is all about. Actually, baseball ranks third with me in terms of the importance of handling pressure.

You can self-inflict pressure. I was always known as being arrogant and cocky. Well, I guess that was my personality coming out, because I wanted to be seen, and wanted to make an impact in certain situations. As a result, I was often told, "You know, you're too cocky. Go sit down." I'd then say, "Well coach, I'm better than that other guy." A lot of times it was taken as arrogance. But then again, in those days, if I didn't think I could do something, I wouldn't have said what I said.

There's a fine line between arrogance and confidence. Arrogance is when someone chirps off at the mouth constantly. On the other hand, when I believed I could do something, I said it and then tried to back it up as best I could. Maybe that was perceived a little differently, but to me it was confidence. That's an example of self-inflicted pressure. There are times when people look at you—and maybe it has nothing to do with you personally—and they think of you as just a blowhard. Their perception might be wrong; but it doesn't matter, because at that point, you've crossed into a realm of outside pressure brought on by yourself.

When I got to Arizona State after high school, I walked on without a scholarship. I walked on to the junior varsity, where there were something like two hundred walk-ons trying out for the team. With two hundred walk-ons out there, they needed eight cuts to get the squad trimmed down to size.

My roommate at that time was Ken Gabriel, who likewise had walked on. The two of us did almost everything exactly the same. We were both about the same size, quick, and threw and batted left-handed. A lot of times, the junior varsity coach would get confused and get us mixed up with each other. As you can tell, it wasn't the type of situation that breeds a ton of confidence in you. But it was a learning experience for me that proved invaluable.

We ended up working out with some of the varsity players who obviously weren't going to see a lot of varsity action that year. That's how I became good friends with guys like Chris Bando. Those of you who are baseball fans should recognize a lot of the names of guys who were then at Arizona State (1976) and whom I got to know: catcher Gary Allenson, first baseman Kenny Phelps, second baseman Ricky Peters, infielder Bob Horner (then a shortstop), third baseman Chris Nyman, outfielders Bobby Pate and Kenny Landreaux, and pitchers Floyd Bannister and Darrell Jackson. Out of the twenty-five or twenty-six guys on that ball club, twenty-one of them eventually got drafted by major-league teams.

Somewhere in there, my roommate and I impressed junior varsity coach Clint Myers enough for us to make it all the way through the eight cuts and onto the team. There were eight of us from that walk-on group that survived the cuts. I stayed at Arizona State only one year before I transferred to Southeastern Oklahoma, a small school that (basketball star) Dennis Rodman attended.

Years later, I discovered just how much of an impression I had made on (head varsity coach) Jim Brock back at Arizona State. When I got to the big leagues, people asked me where I had played my college ball. I would tell them that I had played at Arizona State for one year before transferring to Southeastern Oklahoma. When Jim Brock heard I had said that, he said, "Brett Butler never went to my school. If he had been here, I certainly would have known about it." It took Chris Bando going back to him and saying, "Hey, Coach Brock, Brett definitely was here because he hung out with me the whole year."

Again, I believe it was a miracle that I ever made it to the big leagues, because I was five feet tall and weighed eighty-nine pounds as a freshman in high school. Believe it or not, my best sport in high school was wrestling. Although my ultimate goal was to be a major-league baseball player, and although I loved football—I was a quarterback—my best sport in high school was wrestling. I loved it. By my senior year, I weighed about 146 or 147. But I cut a bunch of weight and wrestled in the 119-pound division my senior year. I was itty-bitty. I was what you call a late bloomer.

Again, I believe it was a miracle that I ever made it to the big leagues, because I was five feet tall and weighed eighty-nine pounds as a freshman in high school.

When I walked on at Arizona to play baseball, I played on the junior varsity team the whole year. But I wasn't on scholarship and couldn't afford school. My dad had said he would pay for a couple years of school and then I'd have to pay for the rest. So later that year, I went home and played in a winter league in Illinois. Still, I couldn't even play for my hometown team in Libertyville because—and this is a familiar story—the coach there also was from Libertyville and knew enough hearsay about me to think he didn't want me playing for him. So I went to Zion, Illinois, about forty-five miles away and played there. I led the league in hitting, and this other guy I knew, Bob Olufs, playing for a rival team in Lake Forest, told me that I could probably get a scholarship to Southeastern Oklahoma.

Let me tell you, I was a city boy. I was born in Los Angeles and raised in Chicago, and here they want me to go down to Podunk U.S.A. So I go down to Southeastern Oklahoma, and I see the coach, Dr. Don Parham, who also was the athletic director. He still is. They call him Doc. My father passed away ten years ago, and Doc is kind of the closest thing to a father figure I now have. When I got there and met him, he started talking about fishing, chicken fried steak, and stuff like that, and I'm thinking, You've got to be kidding. I mean, there's Arizona State with its thirty-five thousand students or whatever, and now I'm visiting a school with about forty-five hundred students. I couldn't help but think, I can't get drafted by a major-league team being from here.

So I went home to Illinois. I was going to write a letter back to Coach Parham, thanking him for the opportunity, but turning him down. Being a born-again Christian, however, I kept thinking there had to be a reason for all this, for why I went there for that visit. One night, I just lay there in bed, not being able to sleep. This was about two weeks before I was supposed to return to Arizona State—you know, just go back out there and try to keep playing there. However, there was something in my heart that said there was a reason for my having visited Southeastern Oklahoma. I got out of bed, woke up my mom, and she says, "I know, you have got to go where your heart says to go." I said, "Yeah, Mom, he (Coach Parham) said they would take care of me. I don't know what's in store, but I've got to go there and find out." So that's where I went. I was fortunate to be a two-time all-American there. I got my degree, and got drafted as a favor to my college coach.

My coach knew a scout from the Atlanta Braves, Bob Mavis, and told him, "This is the best guy I've ever had here, so as a favor to me, would you draft him?" I went in the twenty-third round and signed for $1,000. You know, from the day I decided that I was going to be a major-league ballplayer, there never was a doubt in my mind that I would make it. There were guys I have played with and against over the years, from Little League clear up into college ball and even the pros, who have had more talent than I. But I don't know of anybody who has had any more desire and drive than I have. Maybe a few have had as much, but not more. I ate, slept and drank it. I do that to this day, even though I'm going into my fourteenth year in the big leagues.

In 1979, I was drafted by Atlanta and went straight to Bradenton, Florida, for rookie camp. I was one of two former college players there, mixed in with all these kids eighteen, seventeen, and even fifteen years old from places like Puerto Rico and the Dominican Republic. So there I was, sort of starting over with a new set of challenges at a higher level. About a month later, I moved up to Greenwood, which is A ball with Atlanta, and I finished the season there.

Well, I go to spring training the next year and I'm working out with their AA club in Savannah, Georgia, although they had added some sort of intermediate club in Durham, North Carolina. That's when they brought back the Durham Bulls in the 1980s. Well, I worked out with the Savannah/Durham club all spring training, thinking, Hey, all right baby, I've got a chance to go to Savannah this year. Then at the end of spring training, they read off the Savannah roster and I wasn't on it. Instead, they sent me all the way back to A ball at Anderson, South Carolina. I almost quit. But I decided to hang in there and give it my best shot.

Halfway through the season, I got called up to Durham and finished the year there. That's really where I got my break. I was sent to instructional ball, where I hit .400 and got an invitation to the big-league camp. They needed a leadoff hitter. There was pressure on me there, because Bobby Cox, Ted Turner, Hank Aaron and a bunch of other big names came down to watch. In those four days of instructional ball, I got twelve hits. If I hadn't come through then, I would not have gotten invited to big-league camp. I just wanted to show these guys what I could do. Again, I had put pressure on myself to meet the challenge and had succeeded.

So then I went to big-league camp. But I was the last guy cut. Bobby Cox, the manager, called me into his office and said, "You know, I want to keep you, but they won't let me." Now here I am, up from A ball and at the big-league camp. He then says, "Well, go down and have a good year." And I'm like, "Bobby, you need a leadoff man and I could help you."

Well, God directs us and I knew that God had a plan. I didn't know why he (Cox) wanted me be back down in the minors. So I said, "Where am I going, to Savannah?" And he says, "No, you're going to Richmond." So I skipped Savannah and reported to the AAA team in Richmond, Virginia. I went down there, and to make a long story short, that's where I met my wife, Eveline. She was going to school down there—Virginia Commonwealth. By our third date, I knew she was the one. She had prayed for a Christian man and I had prayed for a Christian woman, and now I know why I went to Richmond.

On August 20 of that year—1981— after the strike, I got called to the big leagues. I finished the season and did okay. But in 1982, I kind of hit rock bottom. I started out with the big club, but struggled and got sent back down. I came back to the Braves and ended up hitting .217 for the year in 240 at-bats. Going into spring training the next year, I knew the writing was on the wall as far as my career with the Braves was concerned. By then, Joe Torre was the manager. Late in the previous season, he had asked me to go to a big bat. Otherwise, I wouldn't stay with the club. I figured I wasn't going to make the team, and that's eventually what I was told in so many words in spring training.

My answer to that was that I was going to go back to my small bat and play so well that Torre would have to keep me. That was my confidence level speaking for me, saying, "I'm going to prove myself again." I ended up making the club. I played in 151 games, hit .280 and then got traded to Cleveland. Before that season, I could have started giving up, but again there was the challenge of proving my doubters wrong.

Even now, every year is a different snowflake. Now it's because I have to prove that I'm not too old. I'll be thirty-seven years old in 1994, and I just read one of those statistical books that points out that Brett Butler has the worst base-stealing percentage in all of baseball. Well, after I get twenty-four stolen bases, I will have five hundred for my career. Hey, you can look at it as my having the worst stealing ratio, but I keep getting around 180 basehits every year. Then someone will counter by saying, "Well, he's getting old and can't keep that up much longer." That's the way it has always been—another challenge, another hurdle. I just believe with the personality God has given me, I've been able to rise above that, and just keep going without ever looking back.

Even now, every year is a different snowflake. Now it's because I have to prove that I'm not too old.

I guess it goes back to my best friend, my dad, saying, "Son, I want you to be able to look in the mirror and tell yourself that you gave your best, whether you succeeded or not. But if you don't give your best and you look at yourself in the mirror, you'll always wonder, Well, if I would have done a little bit more, then maybe I could have made it." I didn't want that. I wanted to give it the best shot that I had.

LOVING WHAT YOU DO:

I'm a baseball fan, and when the 1993 season ended with the Braves in the National League playoffs, I was sitting in the stands watching a game. When I retire from the game, one of my most prized possessions will continue to be this gold card every player gets after playing eight years in the majors. This gold card enables me to get into any ball park for any game, excluding the playoffs, World Series, and the All-Star Game—me and a guest, for the rest of my life, for free.

A lot of guys I play with—when the season is over—don't even want to touch, talk, or hear anything about baseball. But there I am up in the stands with my portable TV on my lap, or watching the game at home. There's Lenny Dykstra doing his thing in Philadelphia and I'm listening in, and then there's Joe Carter, one of my closest buddies, hitting the home run for Toronto that wins the World Series and I'm like, going crazy. I just love the game.

BELIEVING IN GOD:

Obviously, God directed my steps and He enabled me to achieve what I have. It's a miracle. How else could a five-foot, eighty-nine-pound boy who couldn't even make it on his high school team spend fourteen years in the big leagues? Turn the clock back twenty years and picture God coming to me and saying, "Brett, pick your life." My life wouldn't be what it is today, because I probably would have picked less. It probably would have been, "Let me play in the big leagues ten years and make $100,000 a year." I mean, He's blown my socks off.

We have a tendency to put limits on God because of our human frailties. If we would just allow Him to direct our lives, He would take care of us. That doesn't necessarily mean we'll get all the material things we want, because that's not where happiness is found. Happiness is found in a loving relationship with a living God, not with money or fame or whatever. I've had players call me—players who have made millions and millions of dollars, only to contemplate suicide or have gotten to the end of their rope from chasing and drinking and sleeping around, and taking drugs. At some point, they have said, "There's got to be more to life than this." I tell them to build a foundation on a personal relationship with a living God. For me, that is the answer to a successful life.

That's what I try to stress. I can see how He's directed my life all this time. I never really felt like, I've got to do this, or I'm not going to make it. I never felt that. Maybe it was just God having His hand on me.

Also, your marriage has to be grounded in God. You can't do it any other way. I'm not sure of the numbers, but it's almost like 70 percent of all marriages in baseball end in divorce, and out of those that get married again, 50 percent of those end in divorce. It's a shame, but marriages involving a professional athlete have a poor chance of lasting. So I can say, first and foremost, that our marriage is grounded in faith and in our relationship with God. It takes a special woman to be married to a ballplayer. I don't know how Eveline does it—maybe because she has to at times with four kids (Abbi, eleven; Stefanie, ten; Katie, eight; and Blake, six)—but it takes a special woman to pick up and move a home, by yourself with several kids, to the other side of the country and then back again to follow me as I play ball. (Butler lives in the Atlanta area and plays for the Los Angeles Dodgers.)

BALANCING FAMILY LIFE WITH CAREER DEMANDS:

My oldest daughter, Abbi, recently made a comment to my wife, saying, "You know, Mom, all those times I've kidded about wishing I didn't have a famous father? The truth is, I really like it. I like that my dad is famous and that he's Brett Butler, the baseball player."

I've sat down the last couple of years and asked my kids, "Do you want Daddy to retire?" I really did that with the thought that if they said, "Yes, Daddy, we want you to retire," that God had blessed us with the funds to be able to do that. But all three girls—they're eleven, ten, and eight—said, "Daddy, we want you to play as long as you can." The only one who really wanted me to quit was my son, Blake. He's six years old, and maybe he doesn't understand it enough. I want to play long enough that he'll remember it. They've really been in my corner and have been very resilient about it. This has been a normal life for them. They don't know anything but this.

Once we slow down and no longer have two homes in two parts of the country, they're probably going to say, "Dad, our life is boring. We're supposed to be going to spring training now, or we're supposed to be going over here." I mean, I've got a six-year-old son who has accumulated more than one hundred thousand frequent-flyer miles from traveling across the country.

This is our family. Eveline and I last year made a commitment that we wouldn't go more than ten days without seeing each other. While sticking to that promise, we spent I don't know how many dollars flying the family around the country so we could have quality time together. And you know, I talked to them every night on the phone even when we were not together, and they kept me abreast of what was going on and all of that.

You've really got to work at it. To make a marriage and family work, again it goes back to God and having a special wife who can deal with that. You really have to die to self—at least for me. The Bible talks about how women are supposed to be submissive to their husbands. It would be easy for me to love that line and stop reading right there. But it goes on to tell husbands to love their wives as God loved the church. In fact, He loved the church enough to die for it. Think about that. I live for God first, my wife and family second, and I am third. My wife gives me my little honey-do list and I do it. That's how it works, and that's how it should be done.

✳

BRETT BUTLER

Brett Butler has never been a one-dimensional baseball player.

Butler, an All-Star center fielder for the Los Angeles Dodgers, has excelled both at the plate and in the field for fourteen years. He has tormented major-league pitchers with his ability to somehow get on base with either a walk, a bunt single, or a line drive to the outfield. And Butler has been successful getting on base during his career, proven by a career on-base average of more than .370.

Butler has batted more than .300 three times in his career. He has a .290 career batting average, and was closing in on the coveted 2,000-hit mark going into the 1994 season. Once Butler gets on base, he is a threat to steal. In 1993, he stole thirty-nine bases, running his career total to 476.

Butler also does what a leadoff man is supposed to do: score runs. Through 1993, he had scored more than one hundred runs in a season six times and surpassed the one thousand mark for his career.

He is the consummate complete player with defensive skills on a par with his offensive abilities. In 1991 Butler set a National League record by playing 161 games without committing an error. He has also consistently finished among the league's top five outfielders for putouts and assists (throwing a runner out from the field).

Butler has been married to his wife, Eveline, for more than twelve years. They have three daughters: Abbi, Stefanie, and Katie; and one son, Blake.

BRETT BUTLER'S FIVE TIPS ON LIFE AND BASEBALL:
1. If your life is grounded in a personal, loving relationship with God, you will experience true happiness.
2. For a marriage to work, you have to die to yourself and live life for God and your wife.
3. If you don't believe in yourself, nobody else will.
4. If you have a dream, do the very best you can, so when you look in the mirror, there will not be any doubt in your mind that you gave your best.
5. Give 100 percent between the white lines.

Author's royalties donated to Open Door Community

Chapter Three

MARY ELLEN CLARK
O L Y M P I C D I V I N G M E D A L I S T
speaks out on…

PERSEVERANCE:

To persevere means never to give up regardless of the outcomes, good or bad, along the way. There are both failures and successes. Think of these as stepping stones, knowing that you're going to fall off some of them. But to persevere at some things where obstacles pop up again and giving it another shot is what's important. It's working hard for something that you want and seeing the big goal at the end. It's also realizing that there are going to be more goals on a particular day to which you need to pay attention. Each day, each week, each month, each year offers its new set of goals and obstacles. You just keep working through them.

When I started diving, I didn't say to myself, Well, I'm going to be diving for twenty-four years. I just had a goal and however long it was going to take me to do that, that's how long it was going to be. Now that I've reached the goal—the big goal of being in the Olympics and the bonus goal of receiving a medal—the reason why I'm persevering is, again, for the enjoyment of the sport and to challenge myself to reach a higher level. Can I learn the harder dives that the Chinese women are doing, and that the men are doing? It's all about challenging myself from within, and it really has nothing to do with outcome at this point.

I started diving at the age of seven and trained with a Japanese coach, June Andrews. I don't even know how often I was training. It was probably three times a week when I was nine. One of the first road blocks I ran into was when I was nine years old, competing in my first age-group nationals. That was in 1973. I did my first dive into the water, went down and hit bottom, and I broke my finger. I got out of the water and told my coach, "Hey, listen, I think I broke my finger." She was busy coaching my brother up on platform, so I went over to my mom. She was busy socializing with all her friends and she didn't really notice me right away until I put my hand out, almost right in front of her face. It was all crooked, and she exclaimed, "Oh, my gosh!"

After that, I went to the Houston Oilers' doctor. He examined my finger and said, "No, you can't dive." I told him that this was my first nationals and I did not fly to Texas not to dive. I said, "I don't care what you do with this finger, wrap it up, cut it off, whatever. I don't care, but I'm diving." He strongly suggested that I not dive. Of course, I was all in tears because I couldn't imagine not being able to compete and perform. Even at such a young age, I knew enough to know that I had really worked hard. This was the reward, and so I competed at that event. Looking back, that really set the stage for me. Yeah, I was injured, and yes, I wasn't supposed to dive. But to overcome the problem anyway and try to rise to the occasion was my way of dealing with the obstacle.

Another road block was when I was at Penn State and I was totally, completely afraid of platform diving. At this point, we were diving off the ten-meter platform. I told my coach, Bob Goldberg, "Bob, I'm too afraid to do this." He said, "I'm telling you, Mary Ellen, if you would ever try, you'd be really good up there." I said, "Okay."

For me, it was having to face that fear. I remember climbing the ladder, shaking and thinking how this was going to be absolutely nuts! This was a three-story building. There I was, diving off a three-story building, going thirty-three miles an hour and landing in the water, which felt like a brick wall. I thought, Who wants to do this work? Again, looking back at it, had my coach not challenged me by saying, "Mary Ellen, I'm telling you, if you would ever try you could be really good," I might not ever have tried it.

The first time I ever did a dive from up there, I procrastinated fifteen minutes to a half-hour just wondering why anyone would enjoy this frightening activity. As I stood perched on the end of the platform trying to convince myself to dive off, Bob would tell me what to concentrate on and reassure me that I would be okay. After I did the dive, the rush of adrenaline and excitement would encourage me to climb up again. Every time that you do it, you feel more and more comfortable. It's something that's scary at first. Now it's a second home for me.

I share a house with a friend, Julie Bell, but my home away from home is on the platform. You don't get so comfortable that you don't realize the risk that you're taking on a daily basis. I think what's really important to remember every time you go up there is that you have to really appreciate where you are. Yeah, you really are high in the air, and yes, you have to respect the platform and the whole event. It's not something that I take lightly. You can't. You really can get injured.

Penn State was a time of learning platform for me. At that stage of my life, that was my main obstacle. When I was out of school and doing my student teaching, I wasn't training. That was four months of my entire career where I really didn't dive. At that stage I thought, I might be done here; I might retire. I've had a wonderful career; maybe I'll retire and just start teaching. But something in my gut said, No, you really want to try to make the 1988 Olympic Trials and see what you are made of…you need to fulfill this goal and do it.

It was going against what a lot of people might have thought that I should do. After college, everyone was saying that I should get a job. Start my life anew and be done with it. Yet, I was going against the grain. No, I told myself, I really want to do this. I want to keep on diving. Fortunately, I had the support of my family and friends who encouraged me to keep training. So I moved to Orlando, Florida, and worked at a restaurant as a waitress to try to make ends meet. I also worked as a fitness instructor at a health spa. I worked two jobs and trained, and that summer was the first time I made the U.S. National Diving Team. That was in 1986.

Making the U.S. National Diving Team was a major breakthrough. At that point, I was ranked among the top eight in the country and was qualified to travel internationally. I was moving in the right direction. My coach, Denny Golden, soon retired. I called Ron O'Brien. He was coaching at Mission Bay, had a full slate of divers and could not accept me at that time. I then called Vince Panzano at Ohio State, who had been highly recommended, and that's where I went next.

At Ohio State I started going to school to get my master's degree. Once again, I had to make ends meet. A friend of mine sold Cutco knives for a living. I was telling her that I needed a job in between workouts, something that's flexible. She told me I had the personality for it. She said, "You'll be perfect. Call this guy and set up an interview." I did this and the guy, Mike Bella, said, "You're hired!" I started selling knives door-to-door. In a very short period of time, I became the number-one salesperson. Even with that I pretty much gave 110 percent. It was hard work, trying to make a living while also trying to compete on a world-class level in diving, but it was work well worth it.

My winning the National Championship in 1987 was a shock to a lot of people, including myself, because I had barely made the finals, which consists of the top twelve divers. I finished twelfth place in the preliminary contest, which put me in last place going into the finals. In the finals, I dove first, and I just said to myself, I'm going to do one good dive at a time and move on. At the end of the contest, I was national champion and had qualified for the Pan-American Games.

I didn't even know anything about the Pan-Am Games. I was so psyched just having made it to the finals of the nationals. I just couldn't believe it. Like, wow, that's all it took? Just eight consistently good dives? The girl that was leading in the finals, Michelle Mitchell, a friend, ended up failing a dive. Otherwise, Michelle clearly would have won. But things happen. I won and yet it really wasn't a justified

> My winning the National Championship in 1987 was a shock to a lot of people, including myself, because I had barely made the finals, which consists of the top twelve divers.

win. I just felt like, Okay, I did that and it was awesome; but I need to do it again.

The next roadblock was in 1988. That's when I had a problem with dizziness. I went to Australia in January of 1988 and returned with what doctors call benign positional vertigo. When my head was jolted in a certain position, I would become dizzy. This abrupt action would disturb the crystals in the inner ear, making me feel off balance. I had that for about six months and kept on diving through it. That was not a smart thing to do, because at times I would be under water—I have contacts so I can't open my eyes under water—and I would start swimming toward the bottom, thinking that it was the top of the water. That was scary. Whenever I feel that again, or coming on at all, I just don't dive. It's too dangerous. But that's something that I was confronted with and had to overcome in 1988, along with surgery on my left shoulder in November of that same year.

I made it through the Olympic Trials in 1988 and ended up twelfth on springboard and seventh on platform. I didn't make the Olympic team, which consists of the top two divers in each event, but it gave me a really good taste of what the Olympic Trials experience was all about. That's when I made a commitment to keep on trying and to keep competing. I stayed at Ohio State a year after the Olympic Trials, finished my master's degree, and felt that I needed a change. It was time to move away from a college town and into more of a professional environment. I knew Ron O'Brien's program was geared towards that; people under him were working in between workouts and training. I gave him a call and told him that I was interested in making a move, and he said, "Come on down."

I made the move in 1989, when I started training with him. Ron began to take apart every aspect of my diving. His keen attention to details and refinement of skills took me back to the basics as he tried to remold me. When you train for so many years, you have a lot of mistakes that have been ingrained into how you dive. He tried to get rid of them, but by doing that I had to go back to square one. It was like learning how to walk all over again. It's pretty crazy, but that's what he did, and I continue to work on those basics to this day.

There are so many things that have tested my perseverance over the years that I have lost track of some of them. You have to look at each and every one of them as just another little obstacle. However, a lot of people would not want to go through that particular obstacle. They would say, "Forget it," and just run away. For me, every obstacle or every wall, either you can run the other direction or you can hop over. I've always, up to this point, been able to hop over. When it's right in my face, that's when I like to say, "Okay, I can do this and hop over it." Then I do it.

FEAR:

Fear of the activity doesn't really come into it when it comes to competing at meets, because at that point you're there to perform. However, there are times fear becomes a factor in platform diving, especially when you have to deal with certain conditions, like when we train at the International Swimming Hall of Fame. It's located right on the beach. We get a lot of wind, and when you're standing up there and the wind is blowing—sometimes twenty to twenty-five miles an hour—and you need to stay still and perform a dive, it's very scary.

Yeah, your mind can play some serious games on you. That's why it's so important that you concentrate on the positive things.

There are times when you think, Oh my gosh, this wind is blowing right in my face and I have to do a reverse into a two-and-one-half. That's a dive where you are facing forward, but then go back toward the platform. It sounds crazy; and you feel like you have to compensate and change all your techniques, because you think the wind is going to blow you back into the tower.

Yeah, your mind can play some serious games on you. That's why it's so important that you concentrate on the positive things. Maybe the wind is really blowing and you're thinking about how it's really a tough situation here; but you say to yourself, "I need to do this anyway, and what can I think of in a positive way to do a good dive?" In your mind you say, "I need to do this and this, and that's it." It's chasing the fear away. It's facing that fear right then and there. Then when you're in a meet situation, when the wind is blowing and the other competitors are freaking out, you're standing up there going, "Okay, I've done this before." Boom! You're right there in the same situation. Think about a couple of things in a positive way and then do the dive.

For me, it hasn't been so much a fear of failure as it has been a fear of success. There was a period in my life—and I really noticed it in 1991 at the Pan-American Games in Havana, Cuba—when maybe I put too much pressure on myself to succeed. I was very ready for that competition. It wasn't on platform that time. Instead, I made it there on springboard, but I felt really ready. I guess I put too much pressure on myself because I knew I had been to Pan-American Games before and should know how to compete. But I was being unfair to myself by adding pressure, and I didn't do well. I was really disappointed, and I couldn't even speak to anyone about it, because I couldn't believe that I did not dive up to the level I was capable.

I don't know if it was a choke, or if I just didn't rise to the occasion, or if I just put too much pressure on myself, or if I was afraid of success. Maybe I was wondering what would happen if I had done well. Guess what; I would have had to do it again. I talked to my coach (Ron O'Brien) about it, and at this stage I started wondering if it was worth it for me to train another year to be this disappointed. Did I want to train for the Olympic Trials and the Olympic Games? How important was this goal to me? There I was in tears, not knowing if it was worth it for me to train another year and be this disappointed.

Ron said, "Mary Ellen, I think it's worth it to find out if it is worth it. You owe it to yourself to find out. You've been training your entire life for this. You owe it to yourself." At that point, it was almost as if I had to look in the mirror and say, "Okay, something has got to change here, and what is it? What do I need to change?" For me, I think it was knowing and accepting the fact that I deserved success. I knew that I worked so hard for so many years and so long, and yet I hadn't really allowed myself success. I guess I couldn't picture myself up there on the awards platform. Whatever it was, I think I was afraid of success. Because with success comes expectations, and then you have to do it again. I was kind of comfortable hanging around in second, third, fourth, or fifth place.

So basically, we mapped out a plan, and Ron said, "This is what I think we need to change this year in training to get where we want to go." Those changes were the difference.

BEING A RESPONSIBLE ROLE MODEL:

Being an Olympian, you're a role model for a lot of people. I have to acknowledge that and say that's a fact and, as far as handling emotions, that in every situation I am representing myself, my work, my coach, the City of Fort Lauderdale, and my hometown and family. So I try to handle my emotions in a positive way. In that, when something isn't right or I'm stressed from whatever it is, I try to deal with it in the most positive way, or I try to let it go before I have to deal with it, or talk to a friend about it.

SETTING GOALS:

You need to set both short-term and long-term goals. Ask yourself what you want to accomplish in the next however many years. If it's the next four years, fine. If it's the next ten years, that's fine, too. Where do you want to be? Where do you see yourself? The intermediate goals? What are the little goals that are going to help you make you get to your long-term goals? That's real important, because that tells you where you're headed.

You have to know where you're headed. You also have to realize that in setting goals you have to be realistic. They have to be measurable in that you have to be able to say, "Okay, I worked out twice every day for this many hours, and this is exactly what I accomplished in trying to reach this particular goal for this meet in learning new dives. Maybe it means keeping a record to track your goals and the progress you make toward them. In diving, it means learning certain new dives and then performing these dives in smaller meets, so that they will be ready to go if and when you get to the Olympics. You can't all of a sudden learn them right before the Olympic Games. That's not going to fly.

It's important to write the goals down so you see them and know what they are. Then you won't forget them. Tell yourself, "This is where I need to be at this stage, or at this time." It's real easy to get sidetracked. To stay on track you need to work and follow your goals on a daily basis. What you really need to do comes down to the physical workout, the mental workout, and the eating habits. For every element of sports, you need to have goals.

✳

MARY ELLEN CLARK

Sometimes the best things come late in an athlete's career. This is definitely the case with diver Mary Ellen Clark.

Clark's diving career didn't take off until she was twenty-nine years old and competing in the 1992 Summer Olympics in Barcelona, Spain. That's where Clark faced one of the biggest tests of her career.

Competing in the platform diving competition, Clark was in second place after six dives with a legitimate chance at the gold medal. But she muffed her seventh dive and fell to fifth place with only one dive left.

But like a true champion, she came through at crunch time, scoring extremely well with a back one-and-a-half somersault, with two-and-a-half twists. Clark's dive was scored high enough to jump her back up to third place, good for the bronze medal.

Clark used the bronze medal as a springboard to more success in national and international events. After the 1992 Olympics, Clark took top honors in five events from the end of 1992 through 1993. In 1993, she finished first in platform diving at the Phillips 66 Indoor National Championships, the U.S. Olympic Festival, the HTH Classic and twice in the Phillips 66 Outdoor National Championships. She also is an eight-time member of the National Team, representing the United States in international competitions. In this span, she has twice been a member of the Pan-American Games team, a two-time member of the World Fina Cup Games, a member of the 1992 U.S. Olympic team, and a member of the National Team for the 1994 Goodwill Games.

Even while continuing her athletic career as a diver on the U.S. National Team, Clark is working as a spokesperson for McDonald's

Corporation in South Florida, meeting people and promoting the sport of diving, as well as representing and promoting the use of Rexall/Sundown Vitamins. Clark earned a bachelor's degree from Penn State, and has a master's degree in education from Ohio State. As the oldest member of the U.S. diving team as of early 1994, Clark has proved that divers in their thirties can compete internationally in a sport dominated mostly by teenagers.

MARY ELLEN CLARK'S FIVE TIPS ON LIFE AND DIVING:

1. Have fun. If you don't enjoy what you're doing, it's hard to be successful.
2. Don't get down on yourself. In diving, it's okay to miss—even the best in the world miss dives. It's important to stay positive and continue to challenge yourself.
3. Make a commitment. In diving, that means learning as much as you can from other divers and coaches.
4. In platform diving, it's real important that you keep your body tight and ready for impact. Otherwise, the water will really pound your body.
5. Trust in yourself, in how hard you work, and in your abilities.

Author's royalties donated to the Women's Sports Foundation

Chapter   Four

WAYMAN TISDALE
N B A   B A S K E T B A L L   S T A R
speaks out on...

KNOWING RIGHT FROM WRONG:

It's been important to me to stay firm. That was instilled in me a long time ago when I was growing up. It's just been something that my parents always tried to tell me about. Mainly, it goes back to just being myself. Part of being myself is being true to my beliefs. I really don't know any other way. I try to stay on the right track and not deviate from that. It has really been a big help.

When I was growing up, it was just as hard on me as it was on everybody else. There were guys wanting to go out, hang out and do a lot of other things that weren't right. But I was strong and knew I had to be strong, because I knew I otherwise couldn't go home. My mother and family had very strong beliefs, and they believed in not straying. I got plenty of whippings growing up, and that really taught me a lot. To this day, I appreciate the discipline and sense of values I received from my parents.

Peer pressure was just as evident when I was growing up as it is for today's kids. A lot of the kids were drinking and there were a lot of drugs going around, although not to the extent they are today. But still, that stuff was around and I had to really think about it. One time, while I was in the sixth grade, a friend of mine started pressuring me into doing drugs with him. I knew even then that if I ever got caught, I would probably be homeless today—a very beat-up, homeless guy. My older brothers and everybody else close to me just didn't play life like that. I had a good, firm upbringing. However, just because I have made it in the NBA (National Basketball Association) doesn't mean that my trials are any easier.

One thing I always encourage people about is staying consistent with their living. I tell that to teens: stay consistent in your living and listen to your parents.

One thing that doesn't change is right from wrong. One thing I always encourage people about is staying consistent with their living. I tell that to teens: stay consistent in your living and listen to your parents. Seek guidance not only from your parents, but also seek out good Christian ballplayers as role models. Common sense is going to prevail in the end. I don't care how much wrong you do and get away with. Sooner or later, that stuff will catch up with you.

I will never say that I am perfect, but I try to be a good example at all times, even if it's almost impossible. I try to keep a good attitude in public, and carry myself the way a professional should carry himself, on and off the court. You want to get into a routine of doing things right. This (the 1993-94 season) is my ninth year in the league, and it's safe to say I have learned how to stick to it.

Sometimes, the media can get to you. They try to pick at you and make you out to be something you really aren't, especially when you're losing. That's been really trying at times for me, but I have made it through it so far, and I thank the Lord for that. First of all, you have got to keep a good, balanced head about what you're doing. Otherwise, the devil can really sneak in and catch you off track. Before you know it, you're all the way off in the wrong lane with a bunch of traffic coming toward you.

I have always been taught to have a good, positive attitude about whatever I'm doing. With that in mind, I try to carry out everything that I do to the fullest and work as hard as I can to be the best at what I'm doing. In other words, don't go about doing things halfway. As far as my beliefs go, I've always believed in God. I know that He's the reason why and who I am today. He's why I'm still even around and still in the NBA. I never forget those great qualities about being a Christian, and I try always to apply that to everyday life.

Every morning before I get out of bed, I thank God for everything. Before you go to bed, you want to be sure to say your prayers. That's the kind of upbringing I've had, and I feel very fortunate for that. When you're tested, sometimes you have to flee from the devil. It's tough, because sometimes he corners you. Just because I'm a Christian and a professional athlete doesn't mean that I'm never cornered. If anything, it means I'm cornered even more. You have to resist temptation.

In my younger years, I wasn't as strong in my faith as I am now. You will be tested every day, and you get stronger because of it. When you're young and tested like that, sometimes you mess up. However, when you get back up after messing up, you are a better person. It makes you even stronger and more determined.

When you're young and tested like that, sometimes you mess up. However, when you get back up after messing up, you are a better person.

Repent for any sin that you commit. In professional basketball, for instance, you can start with the language barrier—concerning the obscene language that goes on in the locker room. Sometimes you have to talk to professional athletes in the only language that they understand, and it's tough for a Christian, because sometimes that's not our language. A lot of the guys on my team laugh at me because I try to talk their language, but I don't do it the same way that they do it, and they laugh at me. But that's okay, because I'm getting laughed at for the right reasons. My esteem comes from the Lord, not from whether or not my teammates laugh at me as I try to keep my language clean.

Actually, the other guys have paid me a lot of respect for that. Because I don't like to use profanity as a normal part of conversation, they will say something off-color around me, then grab their mouths and say, "Sorry about that." That makes me feel good, because it's letting me know that I'm getting a point across. Furthermore, a couple of teammates have gotten to where they trust me enough to talk about a lot of things. Some of them say there's no way I could be a Christian, but I say, "Look at me; I'm a sinner also. I don't think I'm any better than you or anyone else." But one thing I do have is the willingness to confess my sin.

I believe there is a God, and that's why I am saved. My teammates are willing to be open to me, so I try to work on them a little bit each day. I don't try to push Christianity on them, although I find them coming to me a little bit more.

A lot of times, they want to know how I got saved and why I always need to go to church. I always tell them that I always go on Sundays. Sometimes, they'll come up to me and say, "If I believe, why do I have to also go to church?" I say it's good to go in and get your battery charged up. If you're a believer and you've always been brought up in the church, you already know how good you feel after you come out of church. The fact that you go to church is more out of religion, but when you go to church and you're in the Lord's house, it charges your battery a lot more, and you have more willpower to go out and be a better person and better athlete. So, it's healthy and very important to go to church; and the Bible says you should go to church. A lot of times they say, "Well, I can watch it at home." It's still not the same.

In the heat of the battle in a basketball game, it's tough, but I am able to keep my cool, even in the toughest situations. Now with so many rules about fighting, you can hold your temper a little bit easier. Naturally, you're going to get upset during the course of the game. There's an eighty-two-game season, and when fatigue sets in, you're going to have times when you're going to get upset; but the Bible says to persevere.

When I went to the University of Oklahoma (in the mid-1980s), so much happened so fast that it scared me. That's when I really had to depend on the Lord, because in a matter of one year I went from being Wayman Tisdale, high school All-American, to Wayman Tisdale, college All-American. There's a big difference. It was the first time ever I had encountered all that national press, with everybody looking at me. Some people probably would have gotten a big head and gone a different direction, but I went back and stayed at church, and did the same things I did growing up. That's what was important to me—going home and being in my father's church on Sunday morning. I could do that because we didn't have practice Sunday mornings. The coach (Billy Tubbs) took note of that. He knew how much I liked to be at church, so he didn't make us practice on Sunday morning. He'd let us practice on Sunday evenings. That was important to me.

Life became a fish bowl for me while I was at Oklahoma. Everything I did, every restaurant I went to, everybody knew about it. Had I not been raised in the right way, I think it would have been a problem. But I didn't have too much of a problem other than being looked at through a magnifying glass.

DEALING WITH LOSING:

I believe I've come a long way as a person. I've experienced a lot of losing since I've been in the NBA. They say losing builds character, so I should have a lot of character by now. I never have been on a real winner, although one team once broke the .500 mark. It's been very tough on me. If you have talent and pride, you don't want to be out there losing every night. If I had not been grounded in the Lord, I would have lost it a long time ago.

People see me out there laughing on the court and having a good time, and they say, "Man, this guy hasn't won yet and he's still having a good time." It's because I'm playing for something greater than just basketball. I'm playing for someone greater than any spectator who ever watches me. That's the way I look at this whole game.

> People see me out there laughing on the court and having a good time, and they say, "Man, this guy hasn't won yet and he's still having a good time." It's because I'm playing for something greater than just basketball.

Whether you're the greatest basketball player in the world or the worst, your status is only temporary. In an eternal sense, we're going to have to depend on something much greater than the talent we've been given down here on earth.

HONESTY:

One thing that has always been a great compliment for me is when people meet me and say, "Hey, this is an honest guy." If you tell someone you're going to be somewhere at a certain time, or that something happened, you had better mean what you say. It's very rare when I tell someone I will be somewhere at a certain time and then don't show up.

I've been involved in a lot of charity games involving NBA players; a lot of them promise to the game's organizers they will show up, when, in fact, they never intend to. That kind of dishonesty leaves a really bad taste in my mouth.

※

WAYMAN TISDALE

Wayman Tisdale is a star basketball player few people really know about.

Despite averaging seventeen points and almost seven rebounds a game during his nine-year NBA career, Tisdale has never reached the status of being a household name.

One reason could be that he has never played on a team that has made it to the playoffs. Such is the plight of having played three-and-a-half seasons with the Indiana Pacers and five-and-a-half seasons with the lowly Sacramento Kings.

Tisdale entered the 1993-94 season having scored more than ten thousand points and grabbing more than four thousand rebounds in his career. Tisdale is the Kings' all-time leading scorer (more than sixty-five hundred points) and is second in rebounds.

At Oklahoma University, Tisdale became the first player in National Collegiate Athletic Association history to be named first team All-America in his first three seasons. Tisdale is the Big Eight

Conference's second all-time leading scorer and was named All-Big Eight three times. He broke seventeen school records and nine Big Eight records during his career at Oklahoma.

After his final season at OU, Tisdale played on the 1984 Olympic gold medal team with stars Michael Jordan and Patrick Ewing, and led the team in rebounding (6.4 rebounds a game) while scoring eight points a game.

Tisdale was the second overall pick in the 1985 NBA draft, taken by the Indiana Pacers. While with the Pacers, he averaged sixteen points a game.

Tisdale and his wife Regina live in Sacramento with daughters Danielle and Tiffany, and son Wayman II.

WAYMAN TISDALE'S FIVE TIPS ON LIFE AND BASKETBALL:
1. Put God first.
2. Listen to your leadership and respect it.
3. Set goals. You can't be playing basketball just because you're tall, or football because you're fast. You've got to have a purpose to keep you going in the right direction. Then, never give up on your goal or goals.
4. Be determined.
5. Keep your focus.

Author's royalties donated to the Wayman Tisdale Foundation

Chapter   Five

ANDY VAN SLYKE

A L L - S T A R   B A S E B A L L   P L A Y E R

speaks out on...

REMAINING FIRM IN YOUR CONVICTIONS:

The things that I believe in and hold to are vastly different from my values when I first got into baseball in 1979. At that time, baseball was the most important thing in my life. It was completely out of proportion. I thought my value was wrapped up in my performance on the field. So when I would have a good day I'd feel good about myself; and when I had a bad day, obviously, I wasn't as good a person then. It really made me search about what was important in my life. That search led me to Jesus Christ.

When that transformation takes place, it's not an instantaneous transformation. It takes time. It takes growth. God is continually chiseling away at our shape, forming and reforming His believers into what He wants and intends them to be. This is obviously for our benefit. In the process of growing, I have tried to renew my mind in a way that is pleasing to God and beneficial for me. I would say the things that I hold strong to are my convictions; and, hopefully, they are in line with God.

I think the big change in my life has been keeping baseball in its right perspective. When you've got the world telling you that you're something special just because you hit a baseball well, or catch a ball well, or run well, you have to be careful not to get caught up in that. The message from God is that you're not special because you do those things. You're special because you're part of His eternal kingdom, or you're not. That realization was a real awakening for me. It's a daily battle for a lot of Christian athletes. I think we have to be constantly reminded that the world keeps on telling us that we are something special, when the reality is that we're nothing but a bunch of scum-bucket, low-life sinners. It's only through what Jesus did in dying for us that changes that perspective in God's eyes.

There are four ways that a believer can grow: prayer; Bible study; fellowship; and worship. You really have to get all those four needs met or else, I really believe, you're not a balanced Christian.

There are four ways that a believer can grow: prayer; Bible study; fellowship; and worship. You really have to get all those four needs met or else, I really believe, you're not a balanced Christian. Part of the fellowship in Bible studies can be really beneficial. It could also be the prayer, or any of the fellowship. If you can do those things through the course of the season with your teammates, then you will continue to grow when you lack one or two of those four ways.

It's awfully easy to be sucked back into the black hole on the earth or the world's ways. It's a battle, and that's why you've got to rely on your teammates.

Self-centeredness...pride, now that's a battle. I don't care if you're an athlete or a housewife. Those things are the core of sin. I don't think an athlete necessarily has more self-centeredness or pride than somebody else, because that is the core of all of us, in nature. Self-centeredness and pride: I want to do what I want to do today, or I'm God today and God is not God today. That's a battle for athletes as well as anybody.

One of the convictions, one of the values or virtues, that I try to hold to is the fact that as a father I have a responsibility to be obedient to what has been given me. Part of that is telling my kids that the message from the world is one thing and it's 180 degrees opposed to what God says. That is a responsibility that I take very seriously. That's really the battle. The battle is the world, which is Satan's free rein, and he's king of it. He doesn't own it, but he certainly runs it. Those messages aren't going to be in line with what God says, so as parents we have to be responsible to our kids and make sure that the message is loud and clear. That message has to be that just because the world is saying one thing, it doesn't make it right.

It's tough. I can remember, as kids, my parents basically saying the same thing and thinking that my parents were old fuddy duds. The thing is, it's not only my personal feeling or belief. Where am I getting the authority from? That's where you can go to the Bible with your kids and say, "Listen; this is what it says and this is why I believe." It's not just something that I and my wife make up in our heads.

I never saw marijuana in high school. I saw some beer drinking, and actually did a little bit of it myself. It certainly wasn't an every-weekend deal for me. Also there were always a few of those (promiscuous) girls out there. It has changed so much since, and for the worse. It is wide open now for high school kids, and that's a scary thought, especially when you have the U.S. government advocating and promoting sexual behavior.

Ask your children the questions, "Do you want to do what is right?" "Do you want to do what is a little tougher?" "Do you want to take a stand?" or, "Do you want to be blowing the way the wind blows, the way of the world?" Those are really the questions. Do what is right, or go ahead and not do it. Doing the right thing is the hard thing. We have to understand what it is first that we're doing right.

Jesus was a confrontational person, but He never directly was confrontational to people. He would never tell them that they needed to believe in Him. He would never tell them that they needed to do things. The great thing about what He would do is that He would always ask questions to someone who'd ask Him a question.

You've got to get kids asking questions. Once you've got them asking questions, you've really got them where you want them, because now they really want the answers. If you just start telling kids what they need to do—especially during the high school, rebellious years—then they're just going to run in the opposite direction. Start asking questions and wait for them to come to you seeking the answers.

You've got to get kids asking questions. Once you've got them asking questions, you've really got them where you want them, because now they really want the answers.

DEALING WITH THE MEDIA:

My fundamental approach to the media is I'm not really concerned about it, whether what is written about me is written positively or negatively. The only thing I'm really concerned about is the truth now. If they want to write something that's negative and it's true, I can accept that. If they want to write something positive that is true, I can accept that. But that doesn't shape the way I feel about my value as a person.

I think if players would recognize that and deal with that they could keep the media in its right perspective. Then they could enjoy the media even more—especially for a baseball player. Having to do that on a daily basis is part of the job of a baseball player. It's not as much a part of the job, I should say, as hitting or throwing or catching a baseball. But it's certainly part of it, and there's no way to avoid that unless you take a stance like Steve Carlton did his whole career, or like George Hendrick did, or whoever the player may be.

So just enjoy it; deal with it. Just remember that most of the stuff that is written is not going to be remembered the next day, when another paper comes out and yesterday's newspaper ends up on the bottom of a bird cage.

I think a lot of times reporters want to know if I am holding true to things I say. They're constantly making sure that the things that I have said in the past hold true in my personal life. Once in a while they'll throw the hook out there to see if they can set it. You have to be careful. Once in a while you've got to put it in your mouth, but spit it back out just to keep 'em honest.

HUMILITY AS A HUSBAND AND FATHER:

As soon as I found out I was humble—how does that saying go?—I told someone I had humility and then I lost it. I told someone that I was as humble as the next guy, so I lost my humility. That, to me, is such a tough subject to deal with, because as soon as I tell someone I'm a humble guy, I'm no longer in that position.

I tell you what, my wife has been ordained by God to keep me humble. I say that in such a positive way, but she really does. She keeps me right where I'm supposed to be. She lets me know when I'm out of control. I don't think I'm out of control very often, but when I start getting too far, she pulls the reins on me. There is no question about it that I think I'm a better husband than when I was the first day that I was married, obviously.

Being a better coach, or employer, or getting more sales, or getting the best deal, whatever the case may be, those are all fine. But the real challenge to me is being a better husband and father. I'm afraid that I don't take enough time in investing in those two areas of my life. The greatest gift you can give your kids is to love your wife. I'm in no position to give eternal life; God does that. I can tell my kids about it, but I can't give it to them. Only God can do that. I can give them the gift of loving my wife. I have control over that.

The greatest gift you can give your kids is to love your wife.

I tell you, if everybody who walks down the aisle did that and had kids, we wouldn't have to worry about gun control or condom use or a lot of other things that the government tells us that we need to do.

ENJOYING LIFE—IN MODERATION:

I enjoy a beer as much as anybody. But I'm certainly going to try to choose my place and time where that's appropriate. I also enjoy a glass of red wine at dinner as much as the next guy. I don't think it's by accident that Jesus' first miracle was turning water into wine. Not only did He turn water into wine, but the greatest vintage during the course of that three-day waiting period was the wine that Jesus made.

It's all part of balance. That is the real battle for a Christian—not to get so dogmatic in certain things, saying, "Gosh, this is just the way it is." To me, a battle is keeping God out of the box. Just don't put Him in the box. Once that's done, you're not going to grow any more. Once He's in a box, there's no need to take Him back out again, because you've already figured Him out. At least you think you have.

WORK ETHIC:

The primary question is, "What are you working for?" or "Who are you working for?" Once you have that in it's right perspective, it's a lot easier to do what is required for your job. No question about it: I'm going to do my best and God will do the rest. That's all there is to it. God wants us to take our vocation seriously. Take the responsibility which has been delegated to us in that vocation.

ANGER:

We're all vulnerable to sin nature. I really believe for women it's gossip they're all bent on, and that's biblical. For women, it's also manipulation. For men, obviously, the weak areas are anger and sex.

So we all have our own sin nature. Mine's anger. I think I'm better at controlling it than I was, but that doesn't mean that it's fixed. It probably never will be fixed. But that's part of the growth and maturing and hopefully, some day, it will eventually be filtered out. Prayer is the best place to start, because you're certainly not going to do it on your own power. I lost my temper with my wife one recent Saturday. The deal was that we were in the car and I just snapped on her. I don't know that it'll be the last time. I certainly hope it is. Anyhow, it made me feel like a heel, to throw a wall up. Tear the walls down.

✳

ANDY VAN SLYKE

All it took for Andy Van Slyke's baseball career to take off was a change of scenery.

Van Slyke started off his big-league career in 1983 with the St. Louis Cardinals. However, the Cardinals couldn't figure out at what position to play him. So he played five different positions, including the outfield, and third and first base during three seasons in St. Louis. This revolving door was removed in 1987 when Van Slyke was traded to the Pittsburgh Pirates (along with pitcher Mike Dunne) for catcher Tony Pena.

It is a trade the Cardinals have regretted. Two years after the trade, Pena left St. Louis as a free agent. Meanwhile, Van Slyke blossomed into an All-Star player for the Pirates.

Van Slyke was an instant star in Pittsburgh. In 1987 he batted .320, hit twenty home runs and knocked in ninety runs. To top it all off, Van Slyke was awarded the club's Roberto Clemente Award, which annually goes to the Pirates' most valuable player. This was just the beginning for Van Slyke.

Through his first seven years with the Pirates, Van Slyke had averaged more than fifteen home runs and eighty runs batted in a year, while hitting over .280. Through 1993, his best year offensively was 1992, when he finished second in the National League batting race with a .324 average to go with fourteen home runs and eighty-nine runs batted in. Van Slyke also has more than 1,200 hits in his career.

While he has been productive at the plate, Van Slyke has excelled in the field. He has five Gold Glove Awards—which are annually given out to each league's nine best fielders—and a career fielding average of almost .980. Van Slyke has led the National League in total putouts and assists two times during his years in Pittsburgh. Going into the 1994 season, Van Slyke had won the Pirates' Clemente Award three times and was named the 1988 National League Player of the Year by *The Sporting News*. Off the field, Van Slyke is generally considered by the media as one of baseball's best and wittiest interview subjects, although he takes life and his beliefs quite seriously. He and his wife Lauri have three children—A. J., Scott, and Jared.

ANDY VAN SLYKE'S FIVE TIPS ON LIFE AND BASEBALL:

1. When someone tells me that I "need to do" something, I always first ask, "Why would I?"
2. Kids should listen to their parents, but parents also should listen to their kids.
3. Always leave home with your "yes" face on, not your "no" face.
4. If you know you don't have a chance to get a hit when at bat, bunt.
5. You need to read my story twice.

Author's royalties donated to Fellowship of Christian Athletes, St. Louis chapter

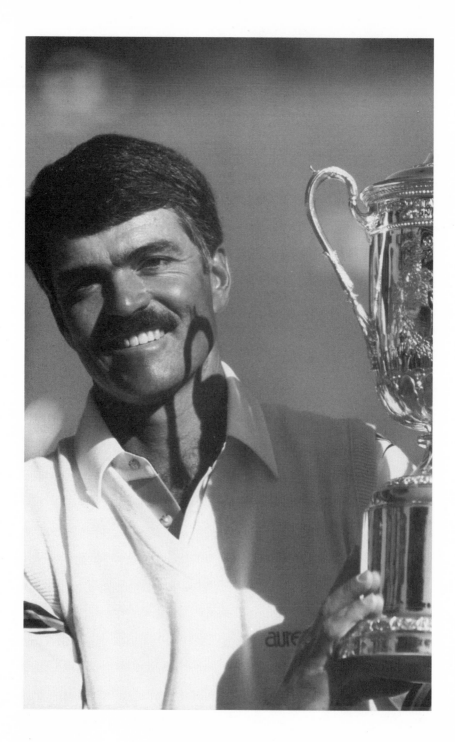

C h a p t e r   S i x

SCOTT SIMPSON
U . S .   O P E N   G O L F   C H A M P I O N
speaks out on...

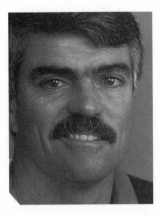

DEALING WITH YOUR EMOTIONS:

I think I've matured a lot in the area of emotions. Growing up, I was really kind of shy, but I was pretty studious. I would try to study the great golfers and see what they did, and invariably, found that all the best golfers can control their emotions. So I realized how important that was; you know, not getting too down when things are going tough and—more important-ly—not getting too excited when things are going well. Otherwise, with emotions that range too wide, you get to thinking about things other than your golf game.

I grew up being a pretty good junior golfer and earned a scholar-ship to the University of Southern California. Later, it took three times before I was able to get through Qualifying School and onto the Professional Golfers' Association Tour. Since making it on tour, things have gone well for me, although I used to have a quick temper. Every golfer who becomes a good player probably has a little bit of a temper that he or she needs to learn to get under control. Still, if you didn't get upset with your bad shots, it would probably be hard ever to improve.

You can't settle for mediocrity if you really want to be one of the best. Almost all golfers tend to be perfectionists. That's where you basically set yourself up for frustration, because there is no way to be perfect at golf. You just can't do it, which is why I think it's so important to control your emotions in golf, maybe more so than in any other sport. I used to have the kind of temper where I would explode. I would get frustrated, and, if things kept going bad, it would just kind of build up until I exploded. I would throw clubs. Most of the time, I would not do that, but sometimes I did.

Almost all golfers tend to be perfectionists. That's where you basically set yourself up for frustration because there is no way to be perfect at golf.

I remember my first year on the PGA Tour (1979). Losing your temper is one of the possible results when you're trying to play well; and, of course, you're trying to play well most of the time you're out there. It could be in front of your home folks. I did it once in front of my girlfriend, who is now my wife. She couldn't believe it. I remember just picking up my bag and throwing it, with clubs going everywhere. I was banging around clubs, even breaking them.

Once, while playing in San Diego, I got really mad at a chip shot I flubbed on the eighteenth hole. I ended up throwing my wedge at my bag, and it actually bounced up and hit playing partner Larry Nelson in the leg. That was one of the most embarrassing things in my life. Larry wasn't too happy. He still remembers it. At the time, he didn't say a lot. But his look pretty much told the story, like "Listen, kid, you had better get your act together if you're going to be out here."

I was just so mad and probably embarrassed that I was doing badly. I think it's a combination of those things that can make you that mad. You almost think you have to do something; so you throw clubs to let everyone know how mad you are—to let everyone know that you don't normally play this badly.

It's been hard for me to control my emotions. My Christian faith has helped a lot in that regard. I've been fined on tour for throwing clubs and stuff, which would probably shock a lot of people, because I have the reputation of being real even-tempered in things. When I am playing well, I am even-tempered. I can take the good and the bad, and have gotten much better at that since I have matured.

I became a Christian in 1984, while I was on tour. Basically, I became a Christian by searching and intellectually discovering the facts about Christianity. In that time, I decided that Christianity really is true as opposed to other religions. Being a Christian has helped me deal with that stuff, because it has put everything into perspective for me. Now I know that golf isn't everything. As a result, I'm able to deal with the bad times better. At the same time, I don't believe that in any way it has taken away from my competitive desire.

I have played some great golf since becoming a Christian, at least as well as before, if not better. Having a walk with Christ frees you up to do the very best you can, because you no longer worry so much about the results. Just go ahead and give it your best shot, and live with it. Choosing to put my faith in Christ has given me hope that there's something more than just this life. Whether or not I become a championship golfer, there's something more to look forward to. You can take pride in the fact that you're doing your best, which is what's really pleasing to the Lord. It's not so much winning or losing as it is behaving in the right way, and handling the good and the bad times in the right way.

> **Having a walk with Christ frees you up to do the very best you can, because you no longer worry so much about the results. Just go ahead and give it your best shot, and live with it.**

In major tournaments, such as the U.S. Open, the emotional pressure is greater because there's more reward for winning something like that. Not only is the money better, but the meaning in terms of tradition and prestige puts more at stake for each golfer. Sure, you're still trying to win other tournaments, but you put a little more into the big ones. Those are the ones where your emotions play a more important role than usual, because that's when you really want to play well. Everyone there is keyed up for the week, and the tendency is to let your emotions get a little more out of control.

One important thing I remember about that week of winning the Open in 1987 was a particular Bible study we had that week. We talked about what it meant to have true contentment in a loving relationship with Jesus Christ. Ever since then, I've gone to the U.S. Open or any other major with the ability to put things in an eternal perspective. Again, your true contentment comes from your relationship with the Lord, with Jesus Christ. It's not going to come from whether you win or lose. Oh sure, the immediate euphoria will be there if you win, but I'm talking about true contentment. With that, I'm able to go out and play with more joy and thankfulness for being there.

One of the key New Testament verses for me in 1987 was Colossians 3:17, which says, "Whatever you do in word or deed, do all for the Lord Jesus Christ, giving thanks through Him to God the Father." That was one of the Scriptures we went over in that week's Bible study. It just describes perfectly the best attitude you could have going out there to play golf. For me, it's being thankful that I'm even there, for one thing. We can take it for granted that it's the U.S. Open and stuff, but boy, there's a lot of good players that aren't there. So I try to remember back to what it was like when I was a junior golfer, watching guys in the U.S. Open and saying, "Wow," and thinking how amazing it would be even to be there. Do it all for the Lord and have an attitude of joy.

When people who might not be believers ask me about this, I try to give them the other side of the coin. Obviously, it's not going to be hard for anyone who wins the Open to say, "Well, I was content all week." Well, who wouldn't be content to win the U.S. Open? But I've had other times, like the next year—1988—when I had missed three cuts in a row going into the Masters, and this was after my best year ever. I went to the Masters and had my brother caddy for me. My mom and dad came to watch me play; and, of course, my wife, Cheryl, was there with me, too. I was working really hard on my game and if ever I wanted to play well, that would have been the time. But I missed the cut again, my fourth in a row. I remember walking off after missing the cut at the thirty-sixth hole, and there were no reporters there. They didn't care.

I remember thinking how I was obviously upset that I didn't play well, but I was also remembering back to the U.S. Open and saying to myself, "Well, it's easy to have contentment then," but I actually did feel content after missing my fourth cut in a row. I wasn't happy, but the true contentment is something deeper inside. I felt that I had given it my best, and I wasn't as upset about it as I normally would have been, because I had given it my best and I knew that the Lord was there with me. It was okay. I still had a lot to look forward to. Contentment comes from keeping things in the right priority, because no matter what we do, we are going to have times when we feel great, and times when we don't. I guess it's just knowing that God is there and that I've got something even past this life to look forward to. Keeping things in their proper perspective helps you always to be thankful and looking ahead, as opposed to getting down and letting your circumstances dictate how you're doing.

I can't think of a great player who is truly a hothead.

I've always noticed that the great players are able to develop that ability to stay on an even keel, when things are going bad or good, and whether they're Christians or non-Christians. I can't think of a great player who is truly a hothead. So, I consciously worked on that a lot. That is probably a process of maturing that has helped me learn to do that better. I think my faith has also helped a lot to make that happen.

EDUCATION:

Both of my parents were school teachers, so getting a good education has always been important in my house. It's so important, because it enables you to go farther and have more choices in what you do in your life. A good education broadens your opportunities as well as the potential for financial rewards, and also gives you the ability to enjoy those rewards.

I don't see anything in the Bible that says there's something wrong with doing well or pursuing excellence. There's nothing wrong with having money. There *is* something wrong with loving money and putting money in front of the things that are so important in life, such as your family and how you approach things. That's why the Bible talks so much about money. There's really nothing wrong with pursuing it, but there is something wrong with loving it and making it your God. We stress academics a lot with our kids and we don't let them slack off. We just keep encouraging them on how important it really is.

MEDIA INFLUENCES:

One of the main things parents need to deal with is their responsibility for what their kids see and hear. We don't let our kids watch every TV show that's on. Also, we don't let them go everywhere they want to go. A lot of the kids in my generation were raised in what was pretty much a permissive society of the 1960s and 1970s. You know, "You don't want to take away anyone's freedom." But my parents believed in discipline and that it was okay to say, "No." It's okay to say, "This isn't acceptable," especially depending on what their ages are. I practice this with my children as well.

So, I guess I put most of the responsibility on the parents. At the same time, there are things that are obscene. While I'm all for freedom of speech, I think it's really important for our country to recognize there are certain things, whether they be obscene or dangerous or whatever, that are not covered by that freedom. I'm really thankful that I became a Christian before my kids grew up, because they have been able to grow up with a Christian value system that will enable them to look at things as they grow older, and be able to say yes or no to them, and probably with a lot more wisdom than I ever had. Hopefully, they will grow up with values that say, "No, I don't want to have sex until I get married to that special person—to save myself— and not to do drugs or whatever."

Don't settle for a good feeling. It's better to wait for the best feeling, and I think that's what the Bible is all about. God doesn't want us to settle for something that's not the best. A loving, committed relationship with your husband or wife is the best, and to raise a family that way is the best. Don't settle for anything less. Our children are learning that, and it will give them a lot more wisdom to make decisions when it comes time to have to make them on their own. They'll have a value system to draw from, besides just going along with whatever or whoever is out there. Raising our kids with a belief in Christ is probably the most important thing we can do for them, for this life and to make sure we'll spend eternity together.

We let our children see most of the movies out there, as long as they're rated G or even PG. We go with them, so that if there are questionable things we will be able to talk to the two of them about it right afterward and ask them what they thought about it. We get into great discussions about it. That can actually be a great teaching tool, too.

As far as TV goes, it's kind of easier now, because there are videos. Our children enjoy watching those, so we have a little more control over what they can watch. We also have a no-TV rule during the week. Besides, they're usually too busy doing their homework. A lot of times they'll have other things they're too busy doing—say basketball, baseball, or something like that—to watch TV.

※

SCOTT SIMPSON

Golfer Scott Simpson has always scored well on the golf course by doing the little things necessary to be successful. Simpson's game is built on precision, not power. Simpson is not a booming driver like John Daly. He does not step up in the tee box and shoot balls into fairways like a cannon. In 1993 PGA Tour events, Simpson ranked 134th in average driving distance.

But Simpson is consistent and is a master around the green. In 1993, he finished among the PGA Tour's top ten in average putts per round. Simpson's consistent, all-around golf game has made him one of the sport's most successful golfers.

Simpson's biggest win was in 1987 at the U.S. Open, contested at San Francisco's Olympic Club, where he outdueled Tom Watson to win the tournament. Simpson won it with clutch play on the last nine holes. He birdied three holes on the back nine to capture his first major tournament title. Simpson almost captured a second Open title in 1991, but ended up losing to Payne Stewart in an eighteen-hole playoff. Going into the 1994 season, Simpson had won five other PGA tournaments. His most recent victory had come in the 1993 GTE Byron Nelson Classic, adding more than $215,000 to his career winnings. Other PGA tournament victories for Simpson include the Western Open, the Manufacturers Hanover Westchester Classic, the Greater Greensboro Open, and the BellSouth Atlanta Classic.

Simpson also has had success internationally, winning four tournaments abroad. Also, in 1987, he was a member of the U.S. Ryder Cup team. Although Scott Simpson might not have the golf game to make people gasp in wonder at his power, he does play golf with precision and accuracy. It has paid off. Through 1993, his career PGA Tour earnings had surpassed $3.5 million.

Simpson and his wife Cheryl have two children: Brea Yoshiko and Sean Tokuzo.

SCOTT SIMPSON'S FIVE TIPS ON LIFE AND GOLF:

1. Put your faith and trust in Jesus Christ. If you do that and follow the Bible, everything else becomes easier. Follow the "owner's manual" of life.
2. Keep learning, whether you're a kid in school or an adult. Keep asking questions. It's fun to learn and expand your horizons.
3. Enjoy life. Don't be afraid to have fun. Life is a precious gift and we don't have much time on earth. Make the most of it, even if it means turning off the TV and playing catch with your son.
4. In golf, make sure the body swings the club, instead of your hands and arms swinging the club. The number-one thing I notice with most amateurs is that they swing too much with their hands and arms, and end up off-balance on their right foot (for right-handers).
5. Enjoy your round and play with what you've got that day. In other words, know your limitations, because they might change from day to day. Many amateurs don't take enough club for some shots. There are days that I can't hook the ball like I like and end up having to play with a fade the whole round. The time to work on your game and do things you haven't tried or might not be comfortable with is when you are on the practice range or golfing by yourself.

Author's royalties donated to Search Ministries

C h a p t e r   S e v e n

TIM SALMON

1 9 9 3   A . L .   R O O K I E   O F   T H E   Y E A R

speaks out on...

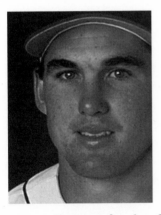

HIS FAITH:

I became a Christian while I was in college at Grand Canyon College, a Baptist school in Phoenix. I went there originally just to play baseball. I am very fortunate that the Lord worked that in my life, because that's where I met Acey Martin. He led me to the Lord, and then I met my wife-to-be Marci there. She has been a Christian her whole life, and comes from a strong Christian family—basically your ideal kind of family.

My coming to the Lord was an evolutionary type process. I look back on that as the biggest time in my life because everything I do today, in one way or another, happens because of the Lord. All my decisions day to day are based upon the things I believe in, mainly my religious convictions and things like that. It is very important to develop that relationship with Jesus through the studying of the word and through your prayer life. During the baseball season, I turn to the Lord more for controlling my emotions and in being able to deal with various circumstances than I do in asking for success. I believe I deal with things in a positive manner, and it all goes back to what I'm called to do as a Christian. That is the number-one priority in my life.

My upbringing was a very rocky road. My parents divorced when I was young. I lived with my mother until I was about ten or eleven, and then lived with my father the rest of the time. I grew up in an alcoholic home. Having seen that kind of thing, I can relate to kids I run into who have been or are in that kind of situation. My brother Mike and I were together the whole time, and I feel thankful for that. He just graduated from USC (the University of Southern California), where he was a football player.

We always believed in God while growing up, but it was not enough of a part of our lives for us to practice our faith diligently. We didn't go to church on Sunday and didn't pray, except in times of struggle or need. I would go to church on Christmas and some other holidays, but beyond that it wasn't something by which we lived our lives. My first real experience with the Lord was when I went to Grand Canyon.

In worldly terms, I can tell you all the reasons for my success, although I know in my heart it's been because of my Christianity. I am where I am because of the grace of God. Obviously, He put me down that road for a reason, and I know that I've learned something from that time. Now that I'm in a situation where I'm often in the lime-light—where people are looking up to me—I believe I can offer them something that's going to bring glory to God.

Athletics has always been such a huge part of life for my broth-er and me. We moved around so much and spent so little time living in each place that we never got to know all of the kids living on the same blocks. But there were always other boys we could play sports with in the interim, playing in things like Little League baseball and YMCA basketball and soccer. We were always athletic year-round, and that kept us out of trouble as we got older. Otherwise, there was noth-ing else keeping us from going down that same road to trouble that a lot of kids go down. It was the discipline we learned from athletics that helped us achieve the goals we have. If we didn't have anybody else, Mike and I always had each other to play toss with or whatever. That was the key.

Anybody who knows me well knows that I'm going to give glory to the Lord for any success I have, whether it be in baseball or anything else. I know enough now to know that I am not in control of the things going on around me. There definitely is a higher source, and it's God. For that, I am thankful.

FAMILY VALUES:

I can see where I have developed some pretty strong opinions about today's world. Tell you what: I fear for my own children, the kind of life they will have to live, and what it's going to be like. I look back on my own life and see my mom, after the divorce, working all the time. Every single day I came home to an empty house. Being the oldest son, and being that there were just the two of us, I was the one who shouldered all the responsibility. I was responsible for the well-being of myself and for my brother. While my mom was out trying to put food on the table, I was seeing firsthand what it was like to live in that kind of a family, without a father who lived with us.

One of the priorities that I have in life is to make sure that my wife is going to be able to be back at home every day with our kids. I want them to have a mother. I want them to have a father. I want them to have a whole family unit that I didn't have. Look at today's society with so many women getting into the workplace. That's great. They're doing things that they can feel good about. But on the other hand, they are the ones who give birth and ultimately are needed the most by children. Children need to have their mother at home with them. They also need to have a father there with them, too. I don't take that lightly.

There are too many problems in society with today's kids, and it goes back to the question, "Where's the family?" There's nobody home when the kids are coming home. I really believe the mother needs to be there for the nurturing and development of the children. I tell my

It was the discipline we learned from athletics that helped us achieve the goals we have. If we didn't have anybody else, Mike and I always had each other to play toss with or whatever.

wife all the time that I am so happy knowing that even if I can't be there at the exact moment when our daughter says her first word, or walks or crawls for the first time, at least Marci is there. You hate to have someone else raising your children and getting to experience all those things. That's something you should want as a parent.

This is one of the areas in which your faith really plays a part. Many people think it's not feasible to live on one income in today's society, but as a Christian I believe that the Lord is always going to provide for you one way or another. Maybe there are a lot of worldly possessions and things that you could do without. It's a matter of what is worth more—being around your children and raising them the way you want them to be raised, or having the expensive houses and cars and all the worldly things. The worldly things are nothing, because they will vanish. It's just a shame that you look at the world today and see so many worldly possessions out there that are just taking away from the family.

> **It's a matter of what is worth more—being around your children and raising them the way you want them to be raised, or having the expensive houses and cars and all the worldly things.**

Where has our society gone? It's gotten to where things like divorce and fathers abandoning their families are not considered "bad" anymore. I guess those fall somewhere in the category of acceptable alternative lifestyles in this day of political correctness. Look at the inner cities, for instance. I had friends in high school who had children out of wedlock, and they don't even see their children. That is such a shame. It says something about the meaning of integrity, which is very important to me.

The responsibility put on me of raising my brother and being responsible for so many things forced me to grow up fast. One thing I learned early on is that when somebody is depending on me for something, it's my responsibility to come through. I have a real problem with going back on your commitments. It's all about integrity. I mean, what are you made of? What kind of man or woman are you? Are you a man of your word? Are you going to stay committed to your wife, remaining faithful?

There are a lot of bad influences out there. Sex is such a big appeal in today's society, and there are so many things out there pulling the man away from his wife and his children, and really confusing him. But if you made a commitment, you really need to stick with it. As a Christian, it is even a bigger commitment because it's a commitment to the Lord. Someone who is not a Christian might not view a commitment as what it really is.

You need to keep things in the right perspective. Baseball is important; it's a game; it's my job; it's my livelihood. But baseball is not more important to me than my family. That's something I remind myself on a regular basis, because it would be easy for me to get so wound up in the game—the ins and outs, and the frustrations and the emotions—that I could lose sight of my family. It's going to be a real test to see how well I do over the years. I really make it a point to keep my family first and above everything else. I don't bring home the frustrations of the game to my wife. There are times when you're really down and you can discuss things and draw support; but as far as coming home and kicking the dog and really causing the family to be in chaos, I try to leave it at the ballpark.

> **Baseball is important; it's a game; it's my job; it's my livelihood. But baseball is not more important to me than my family.**

I just have one child—eight-month-old daughter, Callie. My father-in-law has been a tremendous role model, from the standpoint of being a family man. My wife's family is everything that I would want my family to be. Her father just really is an amazing person. He is a successful engineer and manager of a firm. He is an example of someone who can achieve success without sacrificing his family. To have success in business today, it seems there has to be so much sacrifice on the part of the family. But my father-in-law says it's just putting things in the right perspective and making sure that you have a selfless attitude; put others before yourself.

INTEGRITY:

I believe that I'm a person who doesn't walk around putting different masks on for every person I meet. What people see in me is the way I am. I feel I'm a very fair person. I feel I'm an honest person, even when doing interviews with the media. I find it very difficult doing an interview with someone who tries to categorize me in a certain way simply to formulate a story. I feel very uncomfortable doing that, because that's just not me. I want people to perceive me and to know exactly what I'm about. I don't want there to be any guesswork.

As far as treating people with respect, I always try to treat individuals, such as coaches, managers, or elders, with respect. That type of attitude is biblically based. Discipline has its purpose in that regard. Shoot, in today's society, kids have no respect for authority. This is the case even at ballgames, where kids come at you for autographs. When I was a kid, it was very much, "Yes, sir," or "No, sir," when speaking to adults. But kids today will yell at you and show no respect. They will just shove a piece of paper at you and say, "Sign this." It makes you sick, because you know these same kids are going to become adults who are just out there to get what they can get without any sense of right and wrong.

People might think I'm very square. But I don't lie to people. I don't try to mislead them. There's a right way to do things in life, and I think the biggest testament to that is going to be when my kids grow up and respect me for my integrity. They won't grow up saying, "I saw Daddy ripping someone off at the store," or, "Hey, he really pulled one over on that guy." Marci and I are going to raise our children to behave in a responsible and respectful manner. I don't ever want to be put in a position to jeopardize my integrity, because once you lose it, you lose it. Once you lie to somebody and it's exposed, there will always be that doubt. Integrity in my relationship with my wife means we can have a trustful relationship.

TIM SALMON

Outfielder Tim Salmon was an instant sensation in 1993 for the California Angels. In his first season in the big leagues, Salmon had a monster season at the plate. He batted .283, hit thirty-one home runs, and knocked in ninety-five runs. He also walked eighty-two times and scored ninety-two runs. Salmon did all this in only 142 games en route to winning the 1993 American League's Rookie-of-the-Year award.

Salmon's sensational rookie season also saw him emerge as a defensive whiz. He recorded twelve assists and committed only seven errors. It's little wonder he was named American League Rookie of the Year by several organizations, including the Baseball Writers of America Association, *The Sporting News*, and *Sports Illustrated*. Salmon was also named co-winner—with pitcher Mark Langston—of the team's Owner's Trophy, given annually to the Angels' most valuable player.

Salmon's major league start was no surprise to anyone who saw him play in the minor leagues. While in the minors, he twice hit more than twenty home runs in a season. In 1992, *Baseball America* named Salmon its Minor League Player of the Year. Salmon lives in Phoenix, Arizona, with wife Marci and daughter Callie.

TIM SALMON'S FIVE TIPS ON LIFE AND BASEBALL:

1. You need to have a relationship with God.
2. Maintain a quality relationship with your family and keep them above everything else in the world.
3. Be a man or woman of integrity. Your word is important.
4. Have dreams, goals, and aspirations.
5. In baseball, as with any game, remember that it's only a game and you should have fun with it. If you don't enjoy what you're doing, maybe you shouldn't be doing it.

Author's royalties donated to Unlimited Potential, Inc.

C h a p t e r   E i g h t

STEVE ALFORD
C O L L E G E   B A S K E T B A L L   C O A C H
speaks out on…

FOUNDATIONS:

I have always tried to stay within the guidelines of the game and play the game fairly. I believe in not doing unjust things just to win basketball games. Just follow the rules. The first is understanding sportsmanship. The thing I've probably done best in my career is maintaining a good relationship with people and fans, and particularly the youth in this state (Indiana). I knew I wasn't going to make all the shots, and there would be games where I played very poorly and others where I played very well.

There are a lot of things you can't control in a basketball game. But you can control your actions and your emotions, and that's what I tried to do as a player. Every time I took the floor, I imagined one little girl or one little boy in the stands who was going to do nothing for the entire thirty-two minutes in high school or forty minutes in college but watch me. That really helped me keep things in perspective when things were good or when things were bad. I always knew there were those little eyes watching me.

Sportsmanship isn't something you hear coaches talk about a lot. It's just something that you understand as part of the game, and I think when you're playing with good sportsmanship, you're probably playing better. It's when people lose their emotions and they lose reality about what they're doing that they fail to do things in a sportsmanship-like manner.

I learned a great deal in high school. I had the great opportunity to play for my father and go through that whole relationship. That's not an easy relationship to experience early in your career, being fifteen or sixteen years of age and playing for your father. Not only was I trying to meet those expectations, but also those of my teammates and the entire community of New Castle that I played in front of, because you're tagged as the coach's kid. In that kind of situation, you have different demands and expectations placed on you. Dad pushed me a little bit harder because he didn't want to show favoritism. He expected more out of me, which I really appreciate.

If you don't have the foundation, it's tough to handle the good things as well as the bad. Everybody talks about handling the negatives in life, but a great number of people can't handle the positives as well.

I do about two hundred speaking appearances a year, and the majority of my speaking engagements are to the youth. I always talk about my upbringing in school and the stress caused by the uniqueness of my case, because that is my backbone. I'm a big foundations type of guy. If you don't have the foundation, it's tough to handle the good things as well as the bad. Everybody talks about handling the negatives in life, but a great number of people can't handle the positives as well. They can't keep things in perspective. So they end up changing their beliefs and everything else when good things happen.

My foundation starting forming even before high school because of my relationship with my mother and father, and the relationship I had with my brother. Learning all those relationships have helped me deal with teammates and deal with athletics. My foundation started with the love we had in our family, and then came my acceptance of

Christ while I was a junior in high school. I think you put all these things together—growing as a son, growing as a brother, and then growing as a Christian through high school—and I ended up with a foundation that really helped pave the way for where I am today. With a strong foundation, I was able to accomplish things, not only on the basketball floor, but also from the standpoint of really enjoying everything I was doing.

A lot of young people fail to give any thought to what they hear about knowing right from wrong. They want to explore on their own and do things that burn them once and burn them twice, and then it's too late. They live on excuses rather than saying, "Hey, this is the way things are going to be done. Things are going to get bad for me at school; they'll get bad for me in dating, or relationships; or I'm going to get in a bad situation on the basketball floor or the baseball field. But, if I have a foundation to lean on, I'm not going to crumble under it. I'll be able to pick myself up a lot quicker." That's what our youths really struggle with today—they don't have that foundation, they don't have a solid thing that they can stand on, whether that be a father, a mother, a brother or sister, or their relationship with Christ—having a faith. That's very unfortunate.

A lot of young people fail to give any thought to what they hear about knowing right from wrong. They want to explore on their own and do things that burn them once and burn them twice, and then it's too late.

It's a big problem with our society today. Things have got to start in the home. If a kid has a tough home life, it's very difficult for him or her these days to really build a good foundation. That's why I feel so blessed that I was brought up in a very spiritual home. I was taught right from wrong at a very early age, and really developed a big-time foundation and deep roots that I could lean on in good and bad times. That's why I spend so much of my time with the youths. Even when I'm not out formally speaking to them, I see them from just being out and around, doing little things such as signing autographs. Little kids come up and ask for my autograph, and I sign it. I can remember in college, you would always hear a "Thank you," and now you don't even hear that. They grab the sheet of paper and they go. That's today's standard of common courtesy.

Unfortunately, a lot of those things are being lost. If there's not a home life to go back to, and a mom and dad who are there to set things straight, what does that kid go home to when he leaves school? He goes home to a totally different kind of foundation. Because of our laws, there's no schooling during the week from a spiritual standpoint, and now you've got kids going back home to a home not even spiritual, either. That's got to be tough.

As a coach, I see it even more. It's very difficult to find a player who's going to be able to do the right things when there's a lot of pressure with a lot of people in the stands, and in a situation where the right play has to be executed. When you get a kid who comes from an unstable home and hasn't had a lot of direction, you get a kid who scares you—the coach—to death late in the game when you really have to execute in a pressure-filled situation. There's a direct correlation with a kid that's been taught that foundation at an early age.

The only way to build a good foundation is to rip the old one all the way down and start over, although there are an awful lot of people unwilling to take that risk—to help kids out that way. The great majority of kids don't want to make that sacrifice, either. Yeah, they know that things aren't real good, but they don't want to rip it all down to rebuild from scratch. Really, that's just about the only way you can do it, when you're talking about sixteen to eighteen years of doing things one way, and all of the sudden, somebody's just going to tell you, "Well, that's just not right. This is the way you're going to do it."

But you're still going to have the old habits. It's just like a guy who shoots the basketball with his right hand and he's using his left thumb for eighteen years to help shoot the ball, then all of a sudden you say, "That's not how you do it. This is the way you do it." He picks up that basketball again. He might shoot one or two without that left thumb, but eventually he's going to go back to that old habit. The only way you correct that left thumb usage is to start right at the bottom— at the very elementary steps of shooting the basketball—and take it day by day.

The higher you go in terms of level of competition, the more competitive it gets, and, in turn, the more pressure society puts on winning and losing, and doing whatever it takes to win. I was very fortunate in that I played in a very good high school system. I played at a very good college (Indiana University) where I knew there was no cheating. I also knew players weren't being treated any differently from other students. You can't say that about a lot of colleges. I knew that I was playing for a very honest man (Indiana Coach Bob Knight). I might have disagreed on how he did and said certain things, but the one thing he was, was fair and honest. He just expected our work ethic to be our maximum, whether it was practice or games.

Then I had some very good experiences as a professional playing for John MacLeod (with the Dallas Mavericks of the National Basketball Association) and Don Nelson (Golden State Warriors) as well. So I felt like I was fortunate that I got to play for some very good people and some very good minds in basketball that really helped solidify the foundation that I started on when I was younger.

Being a coach carries a lot of responsibility, and I think that's one of the reasons why I like this position (coaching at Manchester College in Indiana). I can see firsthand the impact that coaches had in my life. If I can in some way, big or small, do that for the players that are playing for me now and in the future, that would feel great. The youth and kids today need as many good examples as they possibly can get, and hopefully I can do a good job in providing one of those.

HAVING A STRONG FAITH:

It's a matter of being bold, like the old cliché of getting off the fence and not straddling it. Many people, when things are going good, will get on the right side of the fence, and then when things get a little heated, they get back up and straddle the thing. Until we as a society really become bold with our faith, and become individuals that are going to be able to take some risks regardless of people liking or disliking what we say, it's going to be very difficult to make any kind of big difference.

What you see in today's church is very unfortunate. The stronghold and the foundation of what Christianity is supposed to be about isn't there. You see a lot of that in churches today. Many people don't attend church now. Others attend church for the first time and end up with a lot of mixed feelings, because they might see an individual in church that they know from work, and find out it's two totally different people.

Being strong in your faith is essential for growth as a person and growth spiritually. If you don't have somebody sharing that with you, whether it's your spouse or your children, or people outside the family, it's very difficult to grow. You need that check-and-balance system just as you need it in coaching and as a player. There were times as a player when I needed somebody to slap me across the head and say, "Hey, you're not working hard enough." There have been times in coaching that I needed another coach to say, "Hey, I disagree with that. I think we need to do this." The same thing happens spiritually.

�֎

STEVE ALFORD

Steve Alford has been a winner in every way in basketball.

After a stellar career at Chrysler High in New Castle, Indiana, he was named Converse's Player of the Year.

For the next four years at Indiana University, Alford was one of college basketball's top players. During his freshman year, Alford was the Hoosiers' leading scorer and was named most valuable player. He also won the Big Ten Conference's freshman-of-the-year award. Later that year (1984), Alford averaged ten points a game playing alongside Michael Jordan and Patrick Ewing on the U.S. Olympic team that won the gold medal in Los Angeles. Alford's next three years at Indiana were very successful as he led the team in scoring and won the team MVP each year.

The 1986-87 season was a magical one for IU and Alford. He averaged more than twenty-two points a game and led the Hoosiers to the national championship. Alford then went on to play four years in the NBA. Each team he played on made the NBA playoffs. His last year in the league was 1991.

Alford began his coaching career at Manchester College in Indiana in 1992. After inheriting a team that went 4-16 in 1991, Alford led Manchester to a 20-8 mark—making for a 500-percent turn-around, the best in NCAA history, regardless of classification. He was named the Indiana Collegiate Athletic Conference Coach of the Year.

Alford and his wife Tanya have a two-year-old son, Kory.

STEVE ALFORD'S FIVE TIPS ON LIFE AND BASKETBALL:

1. You must have a solid foundation in life. It's never too late to start building one, or tearing down the old one and starting from scratch.
2. Have a great work ethic. It takes hard work to be a good player, coach, husband, or father.
3. Love yourself and what you do. It rubs off on those around you.
4. Enjoy what you are doing, and vice versa. We weren't put here not to have fun.
5. In basketball, the foul shot is being continually over-looked. The nationwide percentages this year (1993-94) are the lowest they've been in thirty years. Kids are spending a lot more time on the three-point shot and fail to do anything with the foul shot. A lot of it's concentration and a lot of it is mechanical. The tip I always give kids is there's a nail hole in the floor and I always put my shooting foot on that hole, and that lines up my lower body. Then there's a hole in the basketball that lines up my upper body. If kids would just find the hole in the floor and the hole in the ball, they've conquered a big part of the foul shot in that they've conquered alignment. Now it's going to be very difficult to miss right or left, meaning you've cut down on two of the four ways you miss. (You miss right, you miss left, you miss short, you miss long.)

Author's royalties donated to Blueprint for Life

T R U E
CHAMPIONS

Chapter Nine

MARY JOE FERNANDEZ
W O R L D - R A N K E D T E N N I S P L A Y E R
speaks out on...

KEEPING A BALANCE IN LIFE:

My parents were the key to giving me a balance in life early on. I have an older sister—Sylvia—and I started playing tennis because of her. When I was about three years old, my dad gave me a little tennis racket and told me to go off to the side of the court and start playing, while he worked with my sister. So I grew up with her, and although I started playing tournaments when I was six, and started doing well when I was relatively young—at about ten—it really didn't change anything in the family. I was still treated the same, like my sister, and tennis was just regarded as something extra to be doing, not an end-all in itself.

The main thing for me growing up was to stay in school and get good grades. After I turned pro at age fourteen, there was a lot of pressure on me to drop out of school so I could concentrate on tennis. That's what a lot of my peers were doing, and they were competing quite well. I kept hearing, "You're going to fall behind if you stay in school." But because of my family, and even myself, I actually enjoyed school. I liked going there. School life kept me balanced. When I was in school, I was resting from playing tennis, and when I was playing tennis, I was resting from school. They really complemented each other well. I had to work hard at each one, because I couldn't afford to waste time on either one. In turn, I was forced to learn how to concentrate, which helped me focus and make the most out of my time.

My school was very strict. In order for my school's administrators to let me leave school to play in tournaments—thus accruing more absent days than other girls—I had to get good grades, so I knew that I had to really pay attention in class, do all my homework, and study hard. When I was practicing tennis, I was practicing only an hour-and-a-half or two hours a day, so I really had to focus on that time, because everyone else was practicing four or five hours a day.

That combination of family and school helped me maintain a pretty balanced lifestyle. My parents never let any wins or accomplishments go to my head.

The girls I grew up with knew me before I started playing tennis professionally. So once I started doing well and turning pro—I think it was my freshman year in high school—it wasn't a big deal to them. That also helped me with keeping a good perspective on things. That combination of family and school helped me maintain a pretty balanced lifestyle. My parents never let any wins or accomplishments go to my head.

Looking back, I don't think I was mentally or physically ready to be competing full time—out of school—at such a young age. I think that would have been too much for me. This way, I got the experience, and when I graduated from high school, I was ready and fresh. God willing, I still have a long career ahead of me. I'm sure I was a little bit behind the other girls when I got out of high school because they were playing more, but I don't think I was far enough behind in my development to think there was never a hope of playing as well as them.

Up until two or three years ago, everything was kind of mixed in together. Slowly, I started getting my priorities straight. I believe that if you put your first priority in God, then everything else will follow and everything else will be okay. That's what I try to do all the time, and it's tough, because I compete in a world where people are out there telling you to think about yourself first. But I know that if I really focus on God, everything else will fall into place; your family, your relationships, your friendships, and your career just kind of follow. This doesn't mean you won't have difficulties, because there will always be some coming along. But with God, you know that even the difficulties are okay. In the last couple of years, I have learned to count on Jesus Christ. You can always rely on Jesus.

It's very tough to explain my Christianity to nonbelievers, because it's like you've tasted some kind of food they haven't, and you know how hard it is to describe the taste of a certain food. They would have to experience it for themselves to know it. I'm a big believer in example. Some people are very vocal about it, and I'm not that way. I just figure it's best to be honest and explain what your faith and beliefs are, and how they've affected you.

If you look at it that way—as being blessed with what you have—you won't be so concerned about the result all the time.

I went through a patch in my life where I was definitely putting a lot of emphasis on winning, and it made me very nervous. It took me a while to stop and think, "Why am I getting nervous?" I remember watching the Winter Olympics (in 1994), when they were interviewing (gold medalist speed skater) Dan Jansen. He said one thing his dad had always told him was that life is more than skating around in circles. It's true. For tennis players, life is more than hitting a tennis ball back and forth. It's where your priorities are. You shouldn't focus so much on winning all the time. Just concentrate on doing the best that you can with what you have. If you look at it that way—as being blessed with what you have—you won't be so concerned about the result all the time.

It's good to be somewhat nervous and anxious when you play, but when it prohibits you from playing up to your ability, then it becomes a problem. You start doing well, then expectations get put upon you and you feel like you're supposed to win.

People sometimes ask me, "Don't you get tired of playing all the time? It seems like there's no time for anything else." I see tennis as a very short career. Therefore, I have to take advantage of the time that

I have now and do the best that I can. I want to know that when tennis is over and I retire, that I will have done everything I could with the ability that I was given. I don't know what that is now. I feel like I keep improving, but whether it's being ranked seventh, fifth, fourth, or whatever, it will be fine as long as I know that I gave it my all.

OVERCOMING ADVERSITY:

When you realize you're dealing with adversity, you sometimes feel like, "Gee, why is this happening to me?" Then you remember that other people are going through their own adversity. I've learned that it's actually a good sign if you are going through adversity. It means that God is working in your life, using the adversity to make you spiritually mature. The Bible even says to rejoice in your trials and tribulations. If you see it that way, you kind of rejoice and thank Him that He really has His hand on your life.

Whatever your adversity is, it could be happening for so many reasons. It's hard to say, "Well, why is this happening?" First, I believe God allows adversity; and He uses it to shape us. It could be a way He's trying to produce patience or other character qualities in you. The bottom line is, getting through the problem should make you more spiritually mature. You're now able to deal with life better. But you have to be patient. Give it time. Relax and put everything in God's hands.

Some recent adversity I went through occurred in 1993. I had a really good first six months of the year with my tennis, but then started having some health problems. I was out of the game for four or five months. I had surgery in September, and there I was thinking, "Why is this happening to me? This is the best I've ever played, and now I have to start all over again." I had lost all of the progress I had made in my game during those first six months. I was beginning again and it was very frustrating, because I played a couple of tournaments at the end of the year and it was like night and day. Still, having gone through this, I'm a bit more trustworthy that everything happens for a reason, and I accept it. I thank the Lord that He's working in me.

When you're going through tough times is when you turn more to God. When everything is going smoothly, you kind of ignore Him. That was the lesson that I learned from what happened with me in 1993. The lesson is that you should be looking toward Him all the time and not just when things aren't going your way.

GETTING A GOOD EDUCATION:

I'm very pro education. No matter how good you are in any field, you don't know what's going to happen. Having that good education under your belt always gives you a possibility to do something else.

I love children, and it's sad for me to see people drop out of school. Everybody's different and everybody makes his or her own decisions on it. But I'm a big advocate that you should at least finish high school, because then you can go back to college at any time. For myself, tennis is a short career. What's going to happen when I'm thirty or thirty-five? What if I get hurt and don't have anything to fall back on? That's where my education will help me.

✳

MARY JOE FERNANDEZ

One of Mary Joe Fernandez's many fortes is a never-say-quit attitude, and it has paid off for her in a career that already has been very successful.

Fernandez's perseverance was fully evident in the 1993 French Open quarterfinals. Trailing Gabriella Sabatini 1-6, 1-5, Fernandez was one game away from being eliminated from the prestigious event—one of four Grand Slam events on the professional tennis circuit. But Fernandez never stopped fighting, and the result was a thrilling victory for her. Fernandez rallied in three dramatic sets to win 1-6, 7-6 (7-4), 10-8. The three-hour, thirty-six-minute match was the third-longest in French Open history.

Fernandez showed more of her mettle the next day when she defeated Arantxa Sanchez Vicario in the semifinals, before finally losing to top-ranked Steffi Graf in the French Open final.

While her performance in the 1993 French Open was impressive, Fernandez has been as impressive in many other major events. In singles, she has twice reached the finals of the Australian Open, twice advanced to the U.S. Open semifinals, and made it to the Wimbledon semifinals in 1991. In 1992, Fernandez won an Olympic bronze medal.

Going into the 1994 season, Fernandez had three career victories, including the 1993 Evert Cup in Indian Wells, California, where Fernandez fought off two match points in the final and defeated Amanda Cootzer in three sets. Her other WTA Tour victories were the 1990 Tokyo Indoor Open and the 1990 Filderstadt Tournament.

Likewise, Fernandez has achieved great success in doubles play. She teamed with Gigi Fernandez to win the gold medal in the 1992 Olympics. On the WTA Tour, she has eight doubles victories, including her first Grand Slam victory—the 1991 Australian Open, with partner Patty Fendick.

As of early 1994, Fernandez's career WTA Tour prize winnings totaled almost $3 million. She has finished ranked among the world's top ten women players four times. Off the tennis court, Fernandez enjoys golf, wave running, and water skiing.

MARY JOE FERNANDEZ'S FIVE TIPS ON LIFE AND TENNIS:
1. Put God first and receive Jesus in your life.
2. Put others first. If you do that, things will work out for you.
3. You never know when what you do or say will have an effect on other people, so it's your responsibility to be a good witness. Little things people hear or see can go a long way.
4. Hard work can make up for a lack of talent. Work with what you have.
5. In tennis, I always tell kids it takes a lot of hard work and sacrifices to get ahead. The key is to enjoy it. Have fun out there and don't do anything halfway. Give 100 percent in whatever you do.

Author's royalties donated to The Hunger Project

Chapter Ten

CODY CUSTER

W O R L D   C H A M P I O N   B U L L   R I D E R

speaks out on…

HANDLING SUCCESS AND FAILURE:

After I won the world championship in 1992, I kind of forgot what had gotten me there. As a little kid growing up around the rodeo, I had always wanted to be world champion. But it wasn't until about the middle of 1991 when I started to realize that it was possible I would win the world championship. Then in 1992, everything started off just right for me. I won $7,000 at my first big rodeo of the year, in Denver, but more importantly had reached that point where God was at the center of my life.

Although I wasn't thinking during every waking moment about winning the world championship, it was in the back of my head. I was doing this to glorify God and because of the ability that He had given me. I was enjoying things. I was enjoying life. If I was bucked off the bull, I would still get up and smile, because I knew it wasn't that big a deal.

Then 1993 rolled around. I had won the world championship in bull riding, thus reaching a goal I had had since childhood. Suddenly, my life changed, and so gradually did my priorities. I was quickly swamped with distractions and pressures that were new to me. From the time I got home after winning the finals, the telephone rang non-stop for a week with people—mostly friends—just calling to congratulate me. I really appreciated the thoughts, but it all started to give me a headache.

Before all this transpired, I figured I would get a new belt buckle, then go back to competing without much fanfare. But it wasn't working out that way. The attention was enormous. So I started getting bitter toward people. I would even try to dodge people. It used to be I could just slide into places with the rest of the rodeo crowd, do my thing, take the money and be gone. Nobody would make a big deal over me. Now, suddenly, I was getting congratulated by people I had never met before.

One time, in Fort Worth, I was climbing over the fence and onto my bull in the chute—I was the next rider to go—when some guy tapped me on the shoulder and asked me if he could introduce me to his son. That kind of irritated me. I ended up getting slammed on one jump. I was pretty mad about the whole situation and was dragging my rope out of the arena, when this guy again comes up. I said, "I'll talk to you later," and walked away.

I just started getting blue about being the champ. My riding was slipping. Also, I quit reading my Bible faithfully. I had so much stuff going on. I wasn't cheating on my wife, drinking, or anything like that. However, I was hanging around with cowboys who didn't have the same spiritual goals in mind that I did and was starting to fall back into that worldly attitude like I was somebody important. All along, my keeping God first in my life had allowed me to win the world championship. Not that I was picked by God to win, but by keeping Him first in my life I was able to glorify Him in the best way I knew how. It wasn't really anything I did other than working hard and using the talents that He had given me.

People were wanting me to sign autographs, meet their kids, and all that kind of stuff. I'm not blaming anybody, because I let myself get away from the word of God and from keeping my eyes on Jesus Christ. I was kind of surprised by the direction I found myself headed in. I started realizing what was happening and doing something about it in April 1993. I talked it over with my wife and we started praying about it. My riding had gotten sloppy. I broke my nose twice, suffered a hip pointer, and needed a bunch of stitches in my chin after getting jerked down one time. I was trying so hard to ride not like Cody Custer, but like world champion Cody Custer, that things were going bad, even when I rode decently. I would get off to a bad start, or get run over, and then would have to sit out for a couple of weeks.

Finally, in May, I was working on the Lane Frost movie (*8 Seconds*), doing some of the stunt riding for actor Luke Perry. It was good for me, because I got on a bunch of bulls with no pressure and was really able to concentrate on my riding. But then again, I was still hanging around some guys I didn't need to be around. About mid-May, I broke my nose again and, believe it or not, that was the best I had felt in a long time. My riding was good; the bull just hit me in the nose while I was riding him. Everything felt good and then two weeks later, I tore my biceps muscle loose (on the left arm).

> **I was trying so hard to ride not like Cody Custer, but like world champion Cody Custer, that things were going bad, even when I rode decently.**

I got in a hurry while taping my arm and ended up messing up my arm pretty badly. That was on June 12, 1993. I had to have surgery. At the time, I was starting to get back into the word of God. My riding and everything else was going good. I kept asking God, "Why did this happen to me? Here I am trying to get back into line with you."

After a while, I returned to the locker room. Nobody was around. I just sat down and tears started pouring. I started praying about it. I prayed, "God, show me what this is all about." Immediately, I had peace in my heart. He said, "Just trust me and don't worry about it." It wasn't like He actually spoke to me, but I just had this feeling that it was all going to work out. I got on the phone and called my wife Stacey to tell her I was injured and would have to sit out for a while. Being the prayer warrior she is, she said, "No, I'm not going to accept that." She called one of her church buddies and they started praying. I said, "Honey, I'm not being negative or anything, but this is going to be for the best."

I knew I was going to be out for quite a while because the muscle in my arm was balled up. I flew home the next day and called the doctor, Dr. Pat Evans in Dallas—he's done my knee surgeries and other stuff—and told him what the deal was. I flew down there and he put me back together. I had a surgery a month later on my elbow to clean it out.

My eyes have again been opened and I can see that God put me in this position— not to get movie deals, endorsements, or anything like that. God put me in position with the world championship to tell people about Jesus Christ.

I wouldn't change what happened for anything. Having to stay home was the best thing that happened to me. We had had a baby, Aaron James, in March, so he was almost three months old when this happened.

Well, the busiest time of the year in rodeo is June through September. Those were four months that I would have not otherwise seen my kid but a couple of times. I got to spend time with my wife, my parents, and my brothers. I also got to go to church regularly and get back in the word. My eyes have again been opened, and I can see that God put me in this position—not to get movie deals, endorsements, or anything like that. God put me in position with the world championship to tell people about Jesus Christ. Now, I'm not a forward, vociferous type of guy, but I pray for guidance. I've got a couple of guys on my prayer list, and I've seen a couple of them come to Christ. That's made it all worth it.

In Philippians 4:13 of the Bible's New Testament, it says, "I can do all things through Christ who strengthens me." It goes on to say that it's not me that does it, but Christ in me. A lot of people leave that part of the Scripture out. This doesn't mean that just because you're a Christian, you're going to be able to do everything you want to do. But we can grow and change if we're open to God's leading. That integrity is being an upright person. I know I still have some things I'm working on, and that's the way it's going to be for the rest of my life. That is the way it is with everybody. To be a Christian is not to say you're better than other people, but means you are willing to confess your faults.

When people look at me and say, "There's the world champion," it doesn't really mean much to me. It means more to my friends and family than it ever will to me. My mom and dad are so proud. They put in a lot of time trying to get me down the road learning rodeo, and my success is the greatest thing to them. Dealing with success has a lot to do with integrity and remaining upright. You can't let any junk like fame—not that I'm famous—hinder your walk with Christ. Instead, it should be a motive for us to tell people about Christ.

God didn't cause my injury, but God was glorified out of the deal. This year I'm happy to be back rodeoing and trying to be a guy whom God would be proud of. I will not let my fame or my success in rodeo hinder me from being close to Christ. Anybody who longs to be somebody successful in his career, whatever it is, shouldn't let that hinder him from staying on the straight and narrow. Living my life for Christ and glorifying Him in all things that I did is what got me there. There are many guys who probably ride bulls better than me, but have never won a world championship and maybe never will. Another thing that really gets me is how people change the way they treat you after you become a champion. The guys who are just beginning are the guys who need most of the encouragement. But everybody flocks to the guy who is on top.

DEALING WITH BUMPS AND BRUISES:

Injuries go with the territory. I've been riding since 1979 and have had plenty of bumps and bruises. There are times when I'm darn sore and I don't feel like getting on. But I must keep myself limber. I have a stretching routine I go through. The bumps and bruises are not that big a deal. You've got to do what you've got to do, and this is how I make my living. If I were to worry about all that other knick-knack stuff, I wouldn't do things right. Sure, you have to be a tough guy and all that, but you have to use your common sense at the same time.

If I were to get so sore where I wouldn't be able to perform, then it's time to go home and take a little time off. I've seen a lot of guys go on competing, when they probably should be spending about a week or so at home getting themselves better. In my older age, I'm learning a lot more. You get slammed pretty hard when you're twenty-eight years old; it's not like it was when I was nineteen.

BOLDNESS OF BELIEFS:

I accepted Christ as my personal savior in 1983. I have told many people about it, because it says in the Bible to confess it with your mouth. But to be saying that, only to be chasing girls and drinking, doesn't seem right. I'm not looking down on or judging people who are going through that stuff, but I believe you need to get on one side of the fence and be solid in that. That can be very hard to do, because it's a known fact that Satan is out there to kill and destroy. I don't dwell on that, but I just say it because it's there in Scripture.

One of the Scriptures I often think about says, "Submit to God and resist the Devil; and he must flee." You have to submit to God, and I've seen a lot of stuff happen in my life because of that. It can be tough being a Christian, if you let it be. Still, it's not tough if you walk the straight and narrow. There's a party at every rodeo I go to. There are girls at every rodeo I go to, and the opportunity is there, but I try not to get myself in the position where I would fall. It doesn't matter how good a guy is—if Satan can get you, he's going to get you. He can get you in a position that's going to mess your life up…destroy things if you let him.

I've had several injuries, but nothing real serious. In December 1987, I had knee surgery right after the national finals, so I sat out half the year in 1988. That's when I really got into reading the Word. I was lying there with my leg up and couldn't really do anything else. Once you accept Christ, you should spend time in the Word. That's when things started changing in my life. That was when I decided to abstain from sex. (I wasn't married yet.)

I was a pretty wild kid. I just knew it was wrong every time I had done anything out of line with God's Word for me. After I made that commitment to God, I never did anything like that again until my wedding night. That made me feel good. In turn, that got me started on wanting to understand how God wants me to be.

As far as drinking, I used to drink like a fish. Stuff like that happens around rodeo. You get into it thinking you have to fit in with the guys. A lot of guys start drinking, and that's exactly what I did. All my heroes were like that—at least most of them. But 1988 was the last time I got drunk. I drank a couple of beers the next year and think I had some champagne at my sister-in-law's wedding a couple of years ago.

Alcohol is a drug. It changes your state of mind. If we're faithful to God and listen to Him, He's going to give us some glory. 1st Peter 5:6-7 talks about living your life for Christ. "Humble yourselves under the mighty hand of God, that He may exalt you in due time: casting all your cares upon Him; for He careth for you."

CONFIDENCE:

Bull riding is what I do for a living. It's almost second nature to me, so it's not like I'm going into it each time with my eyes shut. I know what can happen. But I know how to do things right. Every time I get on, I pray for God's confidence. Confidence comes only from God, because there's some bad, old, mean bulls that dang sure will get you, so I don't rely on my own confidence. There are times when my own confidence seeps in and I start getting nervous, but I pray over every animal I get on. Also, I pray beforehand with the guys.

�֎

CODY CUSTER

Bull rider Cody Custer has paid for his success in rodeo.

Custer's price paid has included broken ribs, concussions, knee injuries, a collapsed lung, and a torn biceps.

But Custer has never let the injuries discourage him. All his determination and hard work paid off at the 1992 National Rodeo Finals in Las Vegas. It was there that Custer bucked his way to winning the bull riding world championship.

The world title capped off his best season ever. In 1992, Custer won almost $150,000, making him the leading money winner of the Professional Rodeo Cowboys Association. That year, he also won the bull riding event at the Original Coors Rodeo Showdown.

During his ten-year career, Custer has earned more than $500,000 in winnings. He has won the Dodge National Finals Bull Riding championship three times and is a two-time champion of the Salinas, California Rodeo. Custer's other noteworthy achievements include being honored as the Turquoise Rookie of the Year and being crowned champion of the Turquoise Circuit bull riding competition from 1989 to 1992.

But even with all his accomplishments, Custer knows that each bull ride could be his last.

"There's a lot of danger in bull riding," Custer has said. "It's important to know and remember that you are saved by the grace of God. That's the one thing they (the bulls) can't take away from you."

When he isn't bull riding, Custer spends time with his wife Stacey and son Aaron. His other interests include golf and listening to music.

CODY CUSTER'S FIVE TIPS ON LIFE AND BULL RIDING:

1. Any aspiring bull rider should go to a bull-riding clinic, and learn from somebody who has proven to be successful. Don't go in with your eyes closed. I've seen a lot of kids just jump on a bull without knowing the first thing. Things have changed a lot since the 1950s. The bulls have changed, and so has the equipment. Learn from somebody who has been a champion in the nineties. Still, it's not automatically going to click.

2. When I'm up on my rope—lifting on my rope when the bull's front end comes up—I want to have my shoulders out over the top of that bull's shoulders. That's where the control is. If you're sitting down in on the pockets and leaning back, and your shoulders are behind the bull's, you're going to get all the way back to the rear end. Don't lean back when the bull kicks up. Just sit down and lift on your rope, and that slides your hips up to your rope. When they peek out, that's probably when you should turn loose of your feet.

At most of the schools, a lot of young riders try to just keep their feet in and never move their feet. But you have to be shuffling your feet and riding to the front end, because the bull is always going to be moving forward. If you're not riding forward, you're going to lose control of your feet, because all your weight is right on your rear end. Try to keep your weight up on your legs.

3. You can't be overweight and out of shape to ride bulls. I'm not heavy into lifting weights, but I do lift some to keep toned. Any time anything happens and you're in a storm, you need to have the strength to get yourself out of the situation. If you're not strong enough to lift on your rope and keep your shoulders forward, you don't need to be getting on a bull. If you're a little overweight, you need to drop some weight and get yourself in good form.

4. Traveling partners are very important. Partners who want to go out, party all night, and chase girls are probably not going to have as much success. Some guys do that and are still successful, but I've had more success since I quit acting like that. I travel with Christian guys.

5. Paying attention is real important around rodeo. There's no telling what's going to happen that hasn't been rehearsed. It's a wild thing. A bull might jump the fence and run you over if you're not paying attention. I have tried to get the idea through to young kids that it's a dangerous sport. It doesn't matter if you're in the arena, behind the chutes, or walking in the parking lot. You need to stay on your toes and pay attention to what's going on around you.

Author's royalties donated to Fellowship of Christian Cowboys

Chapter   Eleven

SCOTT FLETCHER
STAR BASEBALL PLAYER
speaks out on...

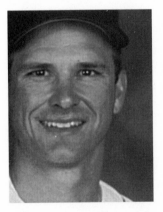

BEING CHRISTIAN AND COMPETITIVE:

Being competitive is something the Lord has taught me about throughout my career as a professional athlete. Over the years, I have heard a lot of people talk about the perception that when somebody becomes a Christian they become complacent, lose his or her drive to win, and things like that. That is totally wrong.

I believe that if you know God and really know how He expects us to go about our jobs and approach the battle, so to speak, people will know that Christians are not complacent when it comes to having a desire to win—a true competitive spirit. One Bible story that really explains it all is the story about David and Goliath. If you read that story you can learn about the way that God would want us to go into the battle or approach our competitiveness on the field.

The Bible says that David was a man after God's own heart. Nothing in this world could get in his way. Now, Goliath was a very big guy, almost ten feet tall, who basically said he would submit his people to any foe that could defeat him in battle. On the other hand, anybody he defeated would have to serve him. So there obviously was a lot at stake. You look at that situation and think, Wow, there was some serious heat there. Can you imagine the President of the United States saying something challenging like that to another nation?

One time when Goliath made his boastful challenge, David heard him and turned to the other men around him, asking why somebody—anybody—wouldn't go up and fight this guy—that this big guy was defying the army of the living God. "I'll go fight him," David finally said. As David approached Goliath, Goliath told him, "I'm going to feed you to the beasts in the field and the fowls of the air." Considering that Goliath had been a warrior from the time he was a youth, you had to figure that not too many people dared to speak back to Goliath when he spoke. The Bible talks about how his presence made people run away in terror. Yet, here David said, "No, I'm going to tell you what's going to happen! I'm going to feed you to the beasts of the field and the fowls of the air, and then after I get done with you I'm going to go get the rest of your people!"

David expected to win that battle. He knew God was with him and that he was going to win. So, David approached the battle; the Bible says he ran toward him. He wasn't intimidated by anything Goliath said. He had great courage. Think about it. Earlier, David had told his king that God had "delivered me out of the hand of the bear and the hand of the lion that tried to steal my sheep. A bear and a lion took my sheep, and I took them and killed them." Just from that alone, you know David had to have some awesome courage.

A lot of times, some Christian athletes new in their walk with the Lord will ask themselves, "Lord, how am I supposed to be out there? How am I supposed to go at it? How am I to approach my job?" The answers to those questions and others are some of the things that the Lord has taught me. He has told me to aggressively go at things: "Be full of courage when you go to the battle."

It's like what God told Joshua in Joshua 1:9: "Have I not commanded you to be strong and of good courage? Do not tremble or be dismayed for the Lord your God is with you wherever you go." So you know that it's not God's will for a Christian athlete to be afraid in the battle. A Christian is not to be passive or afraid. Instead, he is to be full of His courage, with total expectations of winning. Don't be intimidated by the opponent. Be very aggressive, running to the battle. Be willing to take that challenge on, not for your own glory, but for the glory of God. Strive to win and be victorious for the glory of God with the abilities that He has given you. Play to win for His glory that you can tell people that it's His strength, that it's His courage. His Word is alive in you, and has given you that strength and courage to fight on and win.

Jesus often told his disciples to have faith and not be timid or fearful. Faith is the opposite of fear!

Being a competitor with courage certainly applies to being a major league baseball player in today's day and age. Still, you have to be a professional and go about your work right. Play to win, but play fair. You can be competitive without trying to injure someone on purpose or trying to hurt someone else's career. There are rules of the game that you can take a guy out at second base or the pitcher can brush back a hitter. You can play that way. That's just part of the game. You're playing in the game and you're playing it hard; you're playing it aggressively, and you're playing to win.

Play to win, but play fair. You can be competitive without trying to injure someone on purpose or trying to hurt someone else's career.

I try to play very aggressively. Again, that's the way the Lord wants us to be. The motivation to win for God and to give Him the glory is what drives me to go out and play every day. That way, when people say, "How do you do it? How can you keep going all the time? How do you approach it?" I tell them it's because His Word lives on the inside of me. He commands me to be strong and of a good courage. It's His Word that says, "Be strong in the Lord and in the power of His might." It's His Word that says, "Don't grow weary in well doing, for in due time you shall reap if you faint not."

Sometimes when I go to the field, it's like, "Whoa, man, I feel a little weary today; I don't know how I'm going to get it going today."

That's when I keep remembering how the Bible says to keep on plugging. Get yourself ready to go. Do it right for the Lord. That motivates me, strengthens me, and keeps me going.

Everybody is a little different. There are guys who are more quiet. Other guys are a little more emotional. As for myself, I sometimes snap—lose my cool. So do other Christian ballplayers. There are times when I say, "Man, I shouldn't have done that." Nobody's perfect in the field of battle, and that's where you are trying to win. Even if you snap, you can get right back into your fellowship with the Lord, asking Him to forgive you and then keep pressing on. As you mature, you learn that there are situations in which the Holy Spirit can help guide you in keeping your emotions under control. I know a lot of Christians who are good Christians, but will lose it a bit in the heat of competition; but they are thankful that they can come back and say, "Hey Lord, forgive me, let's go again."

> **Nobody's perfect in the field of battle, and that's where you are trying to win. Even if you snap, you can get right back into your fellowship with the Lord, asking Him to forgive you and then keep pressing on.**

I played on a division winner in 1983, during my rookie season with the Chicago White Sox. But we got beat by Baltimore in the American League playoffs. There have been other pennant races since then, but I haven't been on a team that has made it to the playoffs since 1983. As a team player, all I ask for is the opportunity to win the championship and glorify the Lord. So you just keep striving to win that championship.

From a competitive standpoint, if a team is ahead of you in the standings, you just keep on playing hard and keep on going until, hopefully, you wear the other team down and then overtake them. You just keep plugging away professionally the way God wants you to approach it. I think that tells a lot of how God wants us to be and how people can really get a picture of the Lord. That's the whole idea of it. You want people to see Jesus in you. You want them to see God. You want them to see the courage that He gives, the courage that He has.

BEING A ROLE MODEL:

As a professional athlete, I know there are always people watching me, and there is a certain responsibility that goes with that. Athletes should be responsible for their actions and should be role models for all young people. "To whom much is given, much is required."

BEING A TEAM PLAYER:

Teammates need to be able to respect one another, regardless of all the personal differences in things such as personality, background, and experience. It's important for a team to work together. Like the Bible says, "A house divided against itself won't stand." So I think it's important for teammates to be together, to play together, and to keep on working together to win that championship. Sure, certain things flair up or whatever, but they should be quickly resolved in a mature manner. Players should respect and encourage one another, and not point fingers at one another.

Being a team player also means showing respect to your authority. That's not saying you're always going to like the person in that particular position of authority, but you always respect his position. A coach or manager also should show respect to each of his players. There's nothing weak about showing respect.

✳

SCOTT FLETCHER

Infielder Scott Fletcher's versatility in the field and consistency at the plate has allowed him to play twelve seasons in major league baseball. Fletcher has played shortstop, second base, and third base during his career. In that time, Fletcher has committed fewer than ten errors in a season six times and has a career fielding percentage of over .950. His fielding percentage has surpassed .980 four times in his career. Also, Fletcher has always been a solid major league hitter. Despite a relative lack of power from inside the batter's box—Fletcher had only thirty home runs in eleven seasons going into 1994—he has made up for it with clutch hitting and a good average.

In 1993, with the Boston Red Sox, Fletcher batted .285 with thirty-one doubles, five triples, five home runs, and forty-five runs batted in. His value for the Red Sox in 1993 was measurable in other ways, too. It probably was no coincidence that the Red Sox were 65-51 in games in which Fletcher started, yet were 11-31 when Fletcher started the game on the bench. As good a year as 1993 was for him, it wasn't Fletcher's best. While with the Texas Rangers in 1986, Fletcher batted .300 and knocked in fifty runs, followed in 1987 by a season in which he batted .287, hit five home runs, and batted in sixty-three runs. For his career, Fletcher was batting .264 with more than twelve hundred career base hits heading into the 1994 season.

Fletcher and his wife, Angela, have three children (Brittany, age six; Brian, age five; and Brooke, age two). His hobbies include fishing and golf.

SCOTT FLETCHER'S FIVE TIPS ON LIFE AND BASEBALL:
1. Put God first in every area of your life.
2. Love your family.
3. Work hard and never give up.
4. In baseball, keep good rhythm and balance at the plate.
5. Be ready for every pitch, whether at bat or in the field.

Author's royalties donated to Praise Him In Song Ministry

T R U E
CHAMPIONS

Chapter Twelve

DAVID WHEATON
W O R L D - R A N K E D   T E N N I S   P L A Y E R
speaks out on...

THE RIGHT SOURCE
FOR CONFIDENCE:

I grew up in a very strong Christian family and accepted Christ as my personal Savior when I was six years old. My parents gave me excellent, Bible-based training; but, like a lot of "second generation" Christians, I made the mistake of living my spiritual life through my parents, instead of taking hold of it myself.

A few years ago, I began to realize that God will hold me accountable for my own spiritual growth. No one else can do it for me. I am now beginning to understand what Christ means to me personally; and He is impacting my entire life, including my tennis.

The Bible says that we reap what we sow, and I can see how the reality of this truth has played out in my own life. Back in my late teens and early twenties I was riding the fence—spiritually speaking—living my life with one foot in the kingdom of God and the other in the world. Over time, this halfway commitment to the Lord really manifested itself through my life both on and off the court.

When it came to my tennis, I didn't even know why I was playing the game. In fact, I had never thought about it too deeply. I had no firm conviction in my heart that I was playing for the Lord. I might have thought that I was, but deep down I was more motivated by the glory and the money and all the other things that go with worldly success. Somewhere along the line, I began to believe that my success (or failure) would be defined by my win/loss record. So that's where I focused my energies. If something would help me win, I would try it; if not, I didn't have time for it.

The physical part of my game had always come relatively easily to me. God gave me a lot of natural ability and I have trained hard in an effort to get the most from it. In fact, even winning came pretty easily to me throughout my junior and early professional years.

But the mental side of tennis (any sport, actually) is where the real test takes place.

But the mental side of tennis (any sport, actually) is where the real test takes place. After some achievements early in my pro career, my confidence started to suffer as guys found cracks in my game, and I took some bad losses. I think this is when walking both sides of the fence spiritually really took its toll on me.

Between all the coaches I hired and the various sports psychologists I talked with, all I heard about was the power of positive thinking and having a positive mental attitude. They would say, "Believe in yourself," and tell me to repeat to myself, "I'm a winner; I'm getting better every day," and other self-image boosting statements. They showed me examples of how this had worked for many other "successful" athletes.

There I was attempting to apply humanistic psychology to my Christian way of thinking. They don't mix at all—man puffing himself up as opposed to God's way of humility and dependence upon Him. It's like burning a candle at both ends; eventually, it just burns out. It got to the point where I wasn't sure who or what I was supposed to put my confidence in—me or God.

When I was twenty-three years old, I recommitted my life to Christ. I had come to the end of myself and knew that I couldn't try to run my life anymore.

In December 1991 (at age twenty-two), I won the Grand Slam Cup in Munich. It is one of the biggest tournaments in the world and includes a $2 million check for the winner. I remember holding the trophy above my head for photographs and being unable to smile. My brother John was telling me to smile, saying, "David, you just won the Grand Slam Cup!"

For some reason, I had stopped enjoying the game. I thought that going out to practice and play again was a big burden, because I didn't really have any clearly defined purpose as to why I was playing. My feet were on both sides of the fence and it was really the beginning of the end. I had done pretty well up to that point. A lot of people thought that all that money affected me, but that wasn't really it.

All the things that go along with winning a major title like that—the commercials, speaking engagements, and so forth—came along. I got really involved in the business end of it, but I began to lose my focus. A lot of things in my personal life began to fall apart, too. By the end of 1993, I knew there was something drastically wrong in my life. I began a quest to figure out how to have true success in my life.

Being a child of God, I came to realize that human solutions based on human reasoning could not even be part of the answer for me. God has some strong things to say about putting our trust in ourselves instead of in Him. I soon realized that I needed to develop a strictly Christ-centered (not self-centered), biblically based perspective on my life and my tennis.

For my tennis, that's when I knew I needed to learn God's way of developing confidence. Every man who achieved great things for God in the Bible had a clearly defined vision. Most large companies today even have mission statements to define their business. I needed one, too, because up to that point, I had never had one. I didn't have an overwhelming reason for why I was even playing tennis (other than I had played it all my life). I had been somewhat motivated in the past by the enjoyment factor, and the money and the glory. I also wanted to do well for my family. I was motivated by bitterness, as some athletes are today. I've never really been out to prove something to the world. But none of these reasons are good enough for the true

Christian athlete. I knew in my heart that I had to start playing for the glory of God in an all-consuming way.

That's the process I'm in now, and I've only just begun. I'm trying to change my whole perspective so as to glorify the Lord in all that I do. It's been a difficult change, because I had developed habits, tendencies, values, and a certain mindset over the years that were harmless at first, but became harder to break later in life. It will take some time for this transformation to take place as God's Spirit gives me a new, Christ-centered mindset and perspective. In fact, I know it will take an entire lifetime to complete the process.

It's been a difficult change, because I had developed habits, tendencies, values, and a certain mindset over the years that were harmless at first, but became harder to break later in life.

My old perspective—walking both sides of the fence—manifested itself in a number of different ways. One of them had to deal with materialism. To me, materialism is trying to achieve happiness through the money we earn and the things we buy. God gave me that money and He gave me the things that go along with it, but I wasn't looking at it the right way. I was looking at it as though they were my things, and they're really not. As Job said, "We come into the world naked and we leave naked." Everything in between is given to us by God and we are to be stewards of the things He gives us.

Another problem for me was pride. I thought I was in control of my life. I mistakenly believed that I had a good handle on my career and subsequently my success. But I really didn't. Having won a major title, I assumed that I should be able to keep on doing well. Because of these wrong attitudes, however, problems developed in my relationship with my parents. It seemed I could never respond to them in the right way. I wasn't honoring them as God's authorities in my life. If my priorities would have been centered on my spiritual growth first, the other things—my career, relationships, etc.—would have fallen into place. (I refer to Matthew 6:33: "But seek ye first the kingdom of God, and His righteousness; and all these things shall be added unto you.") I was absorbed instead with the worldly benefits that go along with success, when I first and only should have been seeking the Lord.

I don't believe the Bible teaches self-confidence. Instead of having high self-esteem, we should have a high confidence in God. The story in the Bible that best illustrates this for me is the story of David and Goliath. First of all, there's Goliath, who represented the world's way. He was strong, fiercely self-confident, and extremely arrogant (sounds like many pro athletes today!). His defiance of the Israeli army made the Israeli soldiers terribly afraid. The problem was that the Israeli army was matching itself up physically with Goliath. Israeli soldiers were putting their confidence in themselves rather than the Lord.

And then came David, who had been tending his father's sheep. He heard Goliath, and it disgusted him that someone should dare to taunt his God. So David said, "The Lord will deliver me from the hand of this Philistine." Unlike many athletes today, David didn't say, "I'm a mighty warrior, and I'll show the world my skills in defeating Goliath." David's whole focus was to glorify God's name, not his own, throughout the earth. He knew God would honor this, and that's why he put so much confidence and trust in the Lord, instead of himself.

This story is such a good example of having confidence in the Lord. It's not a macho thing at all. It's all about knowing who I am in Christ. When I was saved, I died with Christ to my old, corrupt nature, and now am raised with Him, seated at the right hand of God. So now it's the Spirit of Christ who resides in me. It's not by my own strength anymore.

Galatians 2:20 is one of my favorite verses. It says, "I am crucified with Christ, and it is no longer I who live, but Christ lives in me; and the life which I now live in the flesh I live it by faith in the Son of God, who loved me and gave Himself up for me." It's such a powerful verse, giving us purpose and hope in life. God gives us grace and a supernatural power to do His will. We can have this grace by humbling ourselves before Him, because "God opposes the proud, but gives grace to the humble." Ironically, the gift of grace comes through humility, not through self-confidence, arrogance, or cockiness.

The world believes in your being strong, building yourself up, and making your own decisions. All that is second best to God's way.

It might have temporal results, but will fail under the truly violent storms of life. "Humble yourself in the sight of the Lord, and He will lift you up." When you do that, you can go into any battle you face in life having God's confidence and perspective.

I feel like I'm making progress. The Lord often takes us to the end of ourselves so that we can see our need for Him. At this time in my life, more than any other, I'm hungering and thirsting after Christ's righteousness. I have determined to base my life only on biblical principles, instead of straddling that spiritual fence. God's ultimate purpose for us is stated in Romans 8:29: "For whom He foreknew, these He also predestined to become conformed to the image of His Son." That is true success—being conformed to Christ's image. Focusing on that guarantees success for me, God's way, whether I win or lose a tennis match.

My perspective is definitely changing now. I haven't played a tournament for more than two months (as of February 1994). This is a transitional time in my life, and I'm only in the middle of it. Things still seem a bit confusing to me, though the Lord is helping me understand a lot of things more clearly. I'm having to readjust my thinking in so many ways.

We all need to take in that food every day. There's no other way to grow. Every day, we need to meet with the Lord in a quiet, personal way. As I have learned, no one else can do it for me. There is no place for a passive bystander in the Christian life. Others can certainly help along the way, but I am the one finally responsible for my relationship with the Lord.

HELPING OTHERS:

It's a big responsibility being a professional athlete, because my life is always being scrutinized. It's that way with any public figure. People look at you more and want to see what makes you tick. To really help others, you first need to be where Christ has a good grasp on your own life.

I believe that after salvation comes the need for spiritual growth. Instead of immediately focusing on helping others, it's important to first be grounded in our own personal faith. Then we'll be prepared to help others. As we grow in our daily walk with the Lord, His character will be magnified in our lives, and we can become a great testimony for Him. When you look at the life of Jesus Christ, you don't hear much about the first thirty years. I believe that's because He was preparing Himself for what was ahead in His ministry.

Look, too, at the apostle Paul. He was in the Arabian wilderness for about fifteen years, and some people felt it was wasted time. Not at all. Those were years that Paul was seeking God so he could grow in his faith. It was God working in him so he could then minister to others. His ministry didn't begin immediately after his conversion on the road to Damascus. Sure, he was excited about his new life, and wanted to tell others about it; but his real ministry began after a period of preparation.

FOLLOWING PRINCIPLES:

It's very difficult in our society today. Everyone seems to be living for himself or herself. High moral character is almost a thing of the past, and standards are being redefined to allow for any kind of corrupt behavior. I believe Christ is the only solution. The best thing young people can do is accept Christ as their personal Savior and base their lives on God's Word. The Bible says that God's ways are truth and all of man's ways are vanity. When a young person belongs to Christ, he or she will be able to stand alone, and not succumb to peer pressure and the godless values of our modern society.

A lot of this starts in the family. One of the first things God instituted was the family, and it's the parents' responsibility to train the child in the ways of God. I'm sure glad my parents did, although it took me awhile to personalize my faith.

I recently attended a week-long seminar called "Basic Life Principles." The seminar brings out seven basic biblical principles by which we can live our lives: self-acceptance, clear conscience, authority, meditation on God's Word, moral purity, forgiveness, and yielding rights. I highly recommend this seminar for parents and young people.

⚜

DAVID WHEATON

David Wheaton is a tennis player trying to build on his early successes.

Wheaton, who grew up in Lake Minnetonka, Minnesota, has achieved top-level results at every major tournament. He also has defeated many of the world's best players, including Grand Slam champions Jim Courier, Andre Agassi, Stefan Edberg, Ivan Lendl, and Jimmy Connors.

Wheaton's biggest professional victory came in Munich, Germany, at the 1991 Compaq Grand Slam Cup. He advanced to the finals after beating Germany's own Michael Stich—that year's reigning Wimbledon champion. In the finals, Wheaton defeated American Michael Chang to win the Cup and its $2 million top prize.

Wheaton also has had success in other Grand Slam tournaments, both in singles and in doubles. While advancing to the semifinals of Wimbledon in 1991, Wheaton defeated both Agassi and Lendl. In similar fashion, Wheaton advanced to the singles quarterfinals of both the Australian and United States Open.

As a doubles player, Wheaton has reached the finals of the 1991 Australian Open (with Patrick McEnroe), and the finals of the 1990 U.S. Open (with Paul Annacone).

In addition to his Grand Slam achievements, Wheaton's successes in the Association of Tennis Professionals (ATP) circuit include winning the 1990 U.S. Clay Court Championships and finishing second at both the 1991 Lipton Championships and the 1991 Queen's Club tournament of London. Going into 1994, Wheaton had won more than $1.5 million on the ATP Tour and been ranked as high as twelfth in the world.

Wheaton also had a stellar career before turning professional. He was the United States's No. 1 junior player in 1987 and won the U.S. Open Junior Tournament that same year. In 1988, he was the No. 1 singles player on Stanford University's national championship team.

Away from the tennis court, Wheaton enjoys spending time with his family, when he visits them in Minnesota. He lists ice hockey, water sports, cross-country skiing, and reading among some of his other favorite pastimes.

DAVID WHEATON'S THREE TIPS ON LIFE:
1. Accept Christ as your personal Savior.
2. Make it your life's purpose to be conformed to the character of Christ.
3. Wholeheartedly base your life on biblical principles.

DAVID WHEATON'S THREE TIPS ON TENNIS:
1. Be diligent in working on a well-rounded game. Work on all the shots.
2. Your movement between shots is the most important thing besides actually hitting the shot.
3. Serve more aces.

Author's royalties donated to the Institute in Basic Life Principles

Chapter   Thirteen

DON SLAUGHT
S T A R   B A S E B A L L   P L A Y E R
speaks out on...

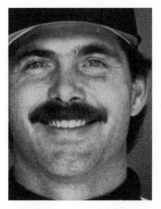

AVOIDING DRUGS AND ALCOHOL:

The speech that I make in front of youth, regarding the use of drugs and alcohol, includes a part where I ask them to hold up their hands if they would answer "yes" to the question, "If I gave you a million dollars, would you stay off drugs for a year?" Of course, all of the kids raise their hands. Then I say, "Well, Steve Howe (a star relief pitcher suspended several times from baseball because of his alcohol/drug abuse) had the opportunity to do that and he couldn't fulfill that obligation. That's how addicting these drugs and alcohol can be."

The message we want to get across to these kids is that using drugs and/or alcohol isn't right. Giving talks like this is something I've been involved with for four or five years, and the need for getting the word out has never been stronger. Even though I'm not really that gifted a speaker, I take part in these assembly programs, because this is something that needs to be done and it's a way for ballplayers as role models to help our youth deal with this aspect of our society. I am unable to make it to every one of these assemblies, but we have several ballplayers in the Arlington, Texas area that we draw from. We take different guys out to each of the different junior highs and high schools, and sometimes even elementary schools, and speak about the cons of alcohol and drugs. Of course, there are no pros; just cons.

The pressures on our youth today are different from the pressures while I was growing up in the seventies. Drugs were available in those days, but the use among children wasn't as prevalent as it is today. On top of that, we now have AIDS. We didn't know what AIDS was when I was back in high school and college. It's no wonder that the pressures that these young people have today are a lot more than what my generation had to combat. So the decisions they make are even more important—especially at early ages. It seems kids are being forced to make these life-altering decisions at earlier and earlier ages. That's why I feel it is important to get our message across.

Ideally, the school-aged children we talk to will already have learned that drugs are bad, and our message would just be reinforcing those beliefs.

Drugs are prevalent in all walks of life. The news is full of people who have thrown their careers and lives away. Ideally, the school-aged children we talk to will already have learned that drugs are bad, and our message would just be reinforcing those beliefs. If you ask my children, ages five and three, what they think about people using drugs, they will say, "That's really bad." They have learned this by Sandy, my wife, and I pointing out examples from news and TV programs regarding how drugs have affected people's lives. They know nothing more than that drugs are bad. But I feel this will at least be their first reaction if ever they are approached.

I was fortunate I never got involved. One of the reasons I never took drugs was because I was afraid I might like them and I knew nothing good could come from that. In high school, I was approached by some friends to try marijuana, but I chose not to. I believe the decision was made years before I was ever approached. For that, I can thank my family upbringing and the solid foundation it gave me with which to make these decisions.

FAMILY LIFE:

I grew up in a Christian family of five children; three sisters and one brother. The relationship of my parents provided us with a strong foundation for our family. Dad worked long hours as a general contractor and developer, and my mom stayed home to raise the kids. My parents provided us with a loving atmosphere in which we were brought up with strong Christian beliefs, and a strong sense of right and wrong. But that doesn't mean I was always such a good kid. In fact, I was a little thief when I was young. It's not something I'm proud of, but is something I admit for the sake of honesty.

I remember stealing a pack of Lifesavers from a store where Mom was shopping. Later on, I was in the closet eating my prize, when my mom caught me. Instead of spanking me or sending me straight to my room, my mom drove me down to the store and made me apologize to the owner. It was a lesson I will remember for the rest of my life. I hope, I will make the effort to do the same for my children.

I guess everyone takes his or her own family as an example, and tries to emulate the good things and make improvements on the bad. I pray that Sandy and I can be as good at being role models to our children as our respective parents have been to us. I see myself in the role of the father as being the Christian leader, the provider, the disciplinarian, the encourager, and the source of love and strength within the family. I feel I grew up in a nice fundamental household, so I have tried to emulate my father.

Discipline is very important within a family, especially when the children are between the ages of two and five years. At that age, they are very impressionable. I believe that is when the majority of their moral values and their learning right from wrong is established. So Sandy and I are pretty strict with our children, or "consistent" might be a better word for it. Our children are taught that sharing is rewarding and lying will get you into the most trouble. I want my children to be able to tell me anything, because I know how many times I have needed my parents' advice in my life. My mother passed on a few years ago, but my father is alive and a great friend. Any time I need advice on anything I call him.

The times I remember most as a child are the times I spent just one on one with my dad, such as when he took me to get a soda after a Little League game, or when the two of us played catch in the park, or when he took me to work with him. This is why I make a special effort to be one on one with my kids. In the off-season, we have something called "buddy day." This was actually started by Sandy. Buddy day is a time when it's just one parent with one child, where we get together for lunch or an activity. This is a great time to communicate without distractions, and to just enjoy each other. The way it works with our kids is that Stephanie doesn't have school on Monday, and Christa has a shortened day on Friday. This gives us an opportunity to be one on one, whether it's doing errands around the city, going to the park, having lunch together, or going to the practice range to hit golf balls. For golf, all you need for a three-year-old is to make a little club and let her swing away. When I was a child, these types of times always made me feel special and important.

I encourage our children to experience a variety of activities, such as gymnastics, dance, soccer, or golf. But we never force them to continue anything if they don't want to. It's important to find some activity that they enjoy and excel at. This builds their confidence and self-esteem, and they also learn the benefits of practice and perseverance. This is what my father did for me, especially when I was young. He let me make choices of my activities. He provided me with everything I needed to participate. I played baseball, football, basketball, and soccer when I was young. In high school, I narrowed it down to football and baseball, and then in college I focused strictly on baseball.

My first catcher's glove was a Ted Williams model from Sears. It cost something like $26, which was really expensive in those days. It was a single-hinge glove, sort of like Johnny Bench's glove, and it wasn't even a birthday present. It was because I was playing Little League that I got this glove. That was the big thing. For anything like that, my father always has gone out of his way to help me. For that, I will be forever grateful.

It's surprising what an influence you are on your children. What I see as the biggest pressure on the family in today's society is the wife having to go to work—the necessity of two family incomes. I am very fortunate in that I make enough money for my wife not to have to work. She has her teaching credentials and she chooses not to work

I feel the greatest thing Sandy and I can do for our children is introduce them to the Christian faith. The second greatest thing I can do is pray for them. Ephesians 6:4 says, "Fathers do not provoke your children to anger, but bring them up in the discipline and instruction of the Lord." It's the father's responsibility to be the spiritual leader within the family. I've made it a priority in my family that we pray together at dinner and bedtime. At my children's ages, we've kept it pretty simple. They know who Jesus is and they know that praying is good. Over the years, we have prayed for their hermit crabs, their boo-boos to heal, the health of our friends and relatives, and their baby brother who's still in Mommy's tummy (as of early April 1994).

The Bible is full of stories about the importance and power of prayer, and I want that power looking after my children. I have tried to stress my priorities to my children as being God first, family second, and baseball third. My parents have had the greatest influence on my life and that is why I take my responsibilities as a father so seriously.

MOTIVATION TO SUCCEED:

When I was a child, I had always wanted to be the first one picked. I had always wanted to be the best. It was an inner motivation. I always have been motivated, but there were three instances in particular where I have made strong commitments to myself and come through.

The first one was when I was in high school and my coach said that I wouldn't make the all-star team. I remember trying out for the California high school all-star game. It was kind of an honor just to get chosen to try out. Before I left for the tryout, my coach told me that if I wanted tickets to go to the game as a spectator, that he would get some for me. I told him that I wouldn't need them, because I would make the team. The funny thing is, I not only made the all-star team and played in the game; I was also named most valuable player of the game.

Later, after I had played about ten years in the major leagues, my high school coach would use me as an example to his students in the classroom, telling them how hard work and motivation could pay off. My high school baseball statistics hadn't really been all that great and it was hard for anyone else at the time to project me as a major league player.

My second story regarding my motivation to succeed concerned my college coach, who said I would never make it as a catcher. He just didn't think I was good enough, and he based his expert opinion on the fact that he had been a catcher in his playing days. I always believed in myself and even used other people's cynicism regarding my talents as a motivational tool. Even after I got drafted by the major leagues, my college coach still said I wouldn't make it as a catcher. But I battled through that and have completed thirteen seasons as a professional baseball catcher.

The third case was when my best friend's dad said, "If you sign a major league contract before getting your college degree, you will never go back to get it (the degree)." It took me three years after getting to the major leagues, but I earned my degree. I kept going back and taking classes. It was a commitment I had made to myself.

FACING YOUR FEARS:

When I hear people talking about the time I got hit in the face with a pitch, they say they would be scared to get back in the batter's box. But I never really had any fear about getting back in the box, because this is something I've been doing since I was seven years old. It was what I did for a living. It's like a race car driver. Even if he gets in a wreck, he's not scared to climb back in behind the wheel. It was circumstances that dictated what happened. I mean, most race car drivers don't quit after they get in an accident. That's because they feel like they're in control.

That's the way I felt when I got back in the batter's box. I felt fine. My statistics went down, but that had more to do with my missing six weeks (during the 1986 season) and bad mechanics resulting from the layoff than it did any fear of the baseball or anything like that. In fact, one of the bigger problems that I had when I came back was experts who kept saying, "You've got to dive into the ball." That was a poor choice of words as far as I was concerned. I started diving into the ball and just couldn't hit. When I go back and look at the replays, I can say now that I just can't swing that way. I was stepping straight toward the plate and trying to swing back toward the pitcher. That's why I went into a slump. I had never hit that way before and there was no reason to hit that way—striding into the plate—anymore. This all took place the next year (1987), and it turned out to be the worst year I have ever had.

BEING A CHRISTIAN AND COMPETITIVE:

Most people perceive Christian athletes as not having any fire. I guess they reach this conclusion when they see a Christian not jumping up and down or ranting and raving when something adverse happens—as if this defines a person's competitive spirit. They're missing the whole idea.

The point is, a Christian athlete really doesn't have a lot of ups and downs, because his self-worth is not based on his performance. This is sometimes perceived as not being very competitive. As a Christian athlete, I like to stay on an even keel. My worth as a person isn't based on whether or not I get three hits today or one hit tomorrow. Sure, I'd love to get three or four hits a day, but I'm not going to get dragged down by a bad day.

I like to believe that a true Christian is a hard worker, a devoted team player, and a man of winning character. I like a guy who competes regardless of the score and is willing to sacrifice for the good of the team.

I like to believe that a true Christian is a hard worker, a devoted team player, and a man of winning character. I like a guy who competes regardless of the score and is willing to sacrifice for the good of the team. Looking at it that way, it should be apparent that being a Christian athlete has nothing to do with lacking competitiveness. A lot of times, the difference between winning and losing is based on the collective character of the team. When a person is struggling, yet keeps going strong, other people can get strength from that. Again, that's where a Christian strong in his or her convictions can be a source of strength.

One of my favorite verses in the Bible is Romans 5:3-6. It says to exalt in your tribulations, knowing that tribulations brings about perseverance, perseverance proven character, and proven character hope. Hope in the Lord and you will not be disappointed. Exalt in your tribulations, knowing that it's going to make you a better person, and make you stronger in character. Any team I play on, I want my teammates to have strong character.

❈

DON SLAUGHT

Catcher Don Slaught has never been a flashy player during his eleven-year major league baseball career.

However, Slaught has almost always gotten the work done and done well. During his career, Slaught—nicknamed Sluggo—has proven to be a clutch hitter and a solid catcher.

Heading into the 1994 season, Slaught had batted .300 or higher three times. And he often has been a batter who comes through in key situations. As a pinch hitter, Slaught was hitting .309 for his career with two home runs and nineteen runs batted in.

In 1993, Slaught batted .337 with runners on base and ended the season with ten home runs, including pinch-hit homers off All-Star pitchers Mitch Williams and Dennis Martinez. For the season, Slaught led the Pittsburgh Pirates with a pinch-hitting mark of .462.

Behind the plate, Slaught has caught more than one thousand games in a career that includes five seasons of throwing out more than 30 percent of base runners trying to steal on him.

Slaught played his college baseball at the University of California at Los Angeles (UCLA). He was the Bruins' captain and was named to the All-Pacific 10 Conference team his junior and senior years. Also, Slaught was named an Academic All-American in 1979 and was named second-team All-America by The Sporting News in 1980.

Off the field, Slaught likes to golf and read, when he isn't spending time with his wife Sandy, daughters Christa and Stephanie, and infant son Cory.

DON SLAUGHT'S FIVE TIPS ON LIFE AND BASEBALL:
1. Pray.
2. Never let others discourage you from the goals that you want to achieve.
3. In anything you do, know that you can always improve. Look at me; as I've gotten older, my stats have gotten better.
4. Always hustle. People will always remember your hustle ahead of your errors or miscues.
5. In baseball, learn to do the "little" things. Those are the things that usually make the difference, i.e. bunting, executing the hit and run, hitting the cut-off man, etc. Mastering those things can make the difference between Triple A and the majors.

Author's royalties donated to Athletes in Action

T R U E
CHAMPIONS

Chapter Fourteen

SUZANNE STRUDWICK

1 9 9 3   L P G A   R O O K I E   O F   T H E   Y E A R

speaks out on...

DEDICATION AND HARD WORK:

I started playing golf when I was eleven and we lived on a golf course in Stafford, England. I became very enthusiastic for the game right away. Living on a golf course, it was very easy for me after school to get out there on the course and play a few holes before it was time to go back in to do the homework and eat dinner. During the summer, particularly with the long evenings, I was allowed to stay up a little bit longer, and I would be out there all the time. I think it sort of got ingrained in me that to produce the results, you need to put in the hard work. From a Christian point of view, I guess a lot of the confidence I have in doing the hard work I do is related to what Jesus said about sowing the seeds—that if you sow the seeds, you're going to reap the harvest. I take that literally; that if you put the hard work in you're going to reap the harvest and that's a big confidence factor for me. On the other hand, if I don't work hard and if I don't practice as much that week, then my confidence is lacking. Although I might be playing well, I find a lack of hard work in practice causes me to be a little bit anxious about my game.

When I started playing almost twenty years ago, I started right out working very hard, and I think that's why my game progressed very quickly. Because of that, I was able to lower my handicap to three by the time I was fifteen years old. That got me into quite a lot of the major amateur events in England. It also gave me the opportunity to represent England in European competition. That was fun, and that's what keeps you going. It was like a circle—once you get more of that higher competition, you get more excitement and adrenaline flowing. As a result, the competition gets to be more fun. And the more fun it is, the more you want to do it. Finally, the more you want to do it, the harder you work and the higher level you are then able to get to.

I probably work harder, or at least the same amount—especially during the summer—as I did when I was thirteen or fourteen. I would be out there on the golf course or practice range, easily eight or nine hours a day. On the range, I would work my short game, my long game, back to my short game, on and on. It didn't seem like work; it was fun. Because the professional golf seasons are so long now, my stamina level has to be quite high. With that in mind, I actually have to force myself to come off the range. That's especially true during the middle part of the season. I want to conserve my energy for the long remainder of the season still ahead. It's a matter of pacing yourself.

One funny instance occurred during the 1993 season, while we were playing in Tucson. I think it was in March. I had already played my round one particular day, after having warmed up on the practice tee for about an hour and a half. Well, I finished my round about three o'clock that afternoon, then went straight to the range. When seven o'clock rolled around, I was still working on my game, hitting shot after shot. A couple of the other girls saw me and literally pulled me off the range and carried me to my car. They'd just had enough of this. I am known as a hard worker. But I think it comes from the fact that I just enjoy it. It doesn't seem like work to me.

Any person who can reach a single-figure handicap has the ability to keep improving. It's all related to the amount of time he or she is willing to put in. When I was playing with a three handicap, I probably could have been content to stay at that level. Perhaps then, I would not have improved as much as I did. Instead, I could have concentrated on, say, wanting to be in business; you know—finish college and get into something else. If I had taken that route, I could have ended up being the age I am now, and then looked back and wondered, Well, yeah, I could have been a pro, but I didn't put enough work into it. It's the amount of work that determines if you can take it to the next level. It demands that much more of an intensity in your practice.

With that in mind, if I were coaching a team, I would hope to be able to make my players want to work harder. I would try to create an environment where it would be fun and they would enjoy themselves. In golf or whatever you are doing—tennis, basketball, whatever—something isn't right if you're having to push people all the time. In that case, you're not creating the right atmosphere for the players to enjoy it enough to want to stay out there and work. I get a lot of enjoyment out of the game and my practice sessions because of the drills, the different things that I do. As a coach or instructor, I would just let my creative mind get into it.

For younger players especially, the range is such a wonderful place to freely do whatever. You can stand there and say, "I'm going to hit ten shots low and fading; and I'm going to hit another ten high and fading, and then ten more low and drawing, and then ten more high and drawing. I'm going to pretend there's a tree in front of me and that I've got to blast it over the top." If you can create an atmosphere where your players are letting their imaginations work, then you don't have to make them work hard. That comes automatically, and generates the fun and the enjoyment of the game.

In golf or whatever you are doing—tennis, basketball, whatever—something isn't right if you're having to push people all the time.

SELF-DISCIPLINE:

I'm very disciplined, and that's gone into the rest of my life. I think being on (the LPGA) tour you have to be disciplined in certain areas, because you have to get things done and there's only a certain amount of time. My willpower is very strong. Before I rededicated my life at the beginning of 1994, I had gotten back into smoking. Then when I rededicated my life, I was able to stop completely right then and there.

I know if I didn't have the willpower that I do, it would have been real hard to quit smoking. It applies to my eating habits as well. I try to follow a good, balanced diet. Yet, on the road, it would be so easy just to stop at a hamburger joint for the convenience and because of the fact you're so exhausted. But I try not to do that! I think growing up at a very early age in the golf environment was helpful in forming my character. It spills over into all other facets of my life.

A big issue, especially with me, the older I get—and I'm not saying that I'm really old at twenty-eight—is my Christianity. After I became a Christian at age twenty-one, I achieved some success in what I was doing. I won a couple of tournaments and eventually was ranked as one of the top five players in Europe. That's when I lost a lot of my dedication to Christ. My perspective on what I was doing was lost in the real world. Golf was my life and it had become my God. The attitude of "Why do I need Jesus in my life?" started to come through. Finally, the Lord definitely brought me to a point where I needed Him. He brought me to the States to play full time, which is something that I had always dreamed of doing. Getting into fellowship with other believers and reading the Bible have given me an understanding of Christ living inside me and shown me how I can live my life in obedience to Him.

HELPING OTHERS:

In coming over here to the United States, I realized that golf isn't everything. There is a lot more to life. In that regard, I'm trying to get my priorities straight. In so doing, I've tried to get into a routine of helping people. That has meant getting into different organizations completely away from golf—opportunities that get you into the real world. A number of us on the LPGA tour built a house at the end of the 1993 season under the auspices of Habitat for Humanity. That was a tremendous experience. We did it around Thanksgiving. Also, there were six of us who went over to Romania for eight days to help out an orphanage, completely away from golf. Here we were, a half-dozen professional golfers, and what we were actually doing had no bearing at all on what we did on the golf course.

That was great, because it shows you that there is an awful lot of need out there. What we do with the money we get through sponsorships, through playing, and through people just being aware can help these people. It was gratifying to do this and build awareness for the cause of these Romanian orphans. It was exciting to see another country, not just in need, but striving to revive itself.

I've traveled overseas quite a bit. I played on the Asian tour for five years. I visited a lot of Asian countries and saw the standard of living over there. That definitely brings you back down to how good we actually have it, even at our lowest point. I just can't understand why a lot of professional sports people, doing something they love, complain when they are going through a bad patch. They complain like crazy about how bad they have it and yet, they are still earning a tremendous amount of money for doing something they enjoy doing. I try to guard against that a lot, and I think doing those kinds of activities, such as building the house and going to Romania, help.

BEING A TEAM PLAYER:

My first team experience was getting onto a national team in England. We had a coach, Vivian Saunders, who is still my coach now. She is tremendous and built a team spirit that I'll never forget. Understand that golf is a very individual sport. Without your even realizing it at first, Vivian could take you to another level. You wanted to play not for yourself. but for your team. If a lot of players had that kind of pressure on them— and it's a completely different kind of pressure— they would do well.

Some don't do well individually, but being a member of a team creates a sort of pressure that you can cope with. On one hand, you know you

Some don't do well individually, but being a member of a team creates a sort of pressure that you can cope with.

have people who are behind you, backing you, believing you and being there to catch you if you fall. On the other hand, you want to show your teammates what you can do. Do your total best and give it 150 percent, because you want your peers' respect and praise. It's the best of both worlds. When you're out there on your own, it's just you, and you're battling against yourself. At that point, it's a matter of being strong and not allowing that little voice inside you to tell you how bad you are or how awful that last shot was. It's just up to you. Your own expectation levels are so much higher than they should be. The pressure mounts and it's just you. So being on a team and having the team spirit is a wonderful atmosphere to have.

Although I wasn't on the Europeans' victorious Solheim Cup team in 1992, I was a part of it because I know all of the European girls very well. I was right in contention to make the team until the last moment. In fact, I was pretty sure I was going to be on the team, so all of us would hang out together for at least two months before the team was picked. We would play practice rounds together. Everything was done as a team and that team spirit carried over. The reason European girls have done so well playing in the United States, especially in 1993, is because of that carryover of team spirit. It has helped their individual games grow.

That confidence level and the high they got out of being on that winning team and backing each other up is something you can't create on your own. I think that's why the Ryder Cup has become so big. The players aren't playing for money. It's a competition against their own peers, and it's trying to gain the respect they want. Of course, you don't want to look foolish or anything if you have a bad day, but you know that the team players are behind you. They're not going to tell you that you just had a terrible day and ask how you could "do that to us." That's not what the team is about.

If I were to get on a Solheim Cup team—and I know Alison Nicholas, one of the other players who was on that 1992 team and who is a Christian—I would like to bring into it a team spirit of it's not winning or losing that matters most. It's taking part in the actual event and enjoying it—that it doesn't have to be some cutthroat, high-pressure situation. Team golf such as that is a wonderful game played in a fantastic environment, with an atmosphere that should be of enjoyment. I would like to think that my actions speak louder than my words and that I could show the other players that, although I'm a Christian, I can be highly competitive and highly motivated to do my very best. I wouldn't want to be some wimp who is wanting to win but who is not being totally aggressive with that.

We are all out there trying to do the same thing. I'm just out there to try to glorify God in what I do. I don't think representing God means merely going out there and playing. It means giving 150 percent and doing the very best I can. It's also saying that if I did my best and still lost, it wouldn't be something that I would carry with me for days and days, and be in some mopey mood. I would then try to uplift the other players and get them motivated to play. People would know that I'm not just out there on my own.

What's recently happened on the LPGA, with many of the other European women playing so well, is the carryover of the team spirit that caught on with the Solheim Cup experience. That team spirit has spread among many of the players and it has continued. It's enjoyable helping each other out and backing each other up. The American women are taking note, not of just our playing ability, but also that we love golf and are out there having a good time.

The American tour is highly successful. It's a stressful, pressurized environment, but we've shown everyone that it can also be very enjoyable. It doesn't have to be a grind.

The American tour is highly successful. It's a stressful, pressurized environment, but we've shown everyone that it can also be very enjoyable. It doesn't have to be a grind. That is the trap that I think a lot of players have fallen into. It's become a grind. That's why many of us from Europe make an effort to take part in other activities together. We play cricket quite a few times during the year. We also play football—soccer—against the caddies that we bring over. We go see things, like when we were in Washington, D.C., quite a few of us went downtown and had a look around, when on the other hand there were players who just never went in to see the city. They wouldn't take the time to do it, even though excursions like that can be refreshing in that they take your mind off golf.

Just being around golf all the time is not good for you. It's not healthy. It's just like that time when the girls dragged me off the range in Phoenix. They could see that I had been out there for too long. I needed something else. Otherwise I was going to burn out.

HONESTY, FAIR PLAY, AND SPORTSMANSHIP:

Golf has definitely shown itself to be one of the most respectful sports for honesty. What happened in figure skating with the Tonya Harding deal shows, unfortunately, how ruthless individual sports can get. It's such a shame. Regardless of Tonya Harding's innocence or guilt, there are certain questions that have to be asked. First, was it worth it? Look at tennis player Jennifer Capriati. She's been through a rough time. She's so young with all that pressure on her. Is it worth it?

In most cases, golf has shown itself to be a sport in which you don't really mature as a competitor until you're in your thirties. It's a sport that takes quite a hard study. By the time you're in your thirties, hopefully realizing your full potential and maturity in golf, you have probably developed the things in your character that would stop you—I would hope—from doing anything too crazy.

STRESS:

The best way to deal with stress is to get yourself out of that environment for a while. Take a couple weeks off, and get your mind occupied on other things so that golf doesn't become the be-all and end-all.

You have to be able to cope with stress, definitely. At the same time, you should be able to live with a certain amount of stress so that you'll push yourself all the time to perform better. It can be a fine line. When it becomes too much, it's time to go and do something else. That's the way I try to deal with it. I enjoy the stress, so I think it's good. A certain amount of it helps me to get motivated. It makes me want to become a better player. It drives me. It's a driving force that keeps me out there.

✳
SUZANNE STRUDWICK

Suzanne Strudwick was a rookie sensation on the LPGA tour in 1993. She competed in twenty-two events, won more than $50,000 in prize money, and capped her rookie year off by winning the Gatorade Rookie of the Year award.

Golfing success is nothing new for the twenty-eight-year-old Strudwick, who is a native of Stafford, England. She competed on the WPG European Tour and won top honors in two events: the 1989 French Open and the 1991 AGF Paris Open. She qualified for the LPGA tour in October, 1992, and has since concentrated her golfing efforts mostly to the American tour.

Strudwick started playing golf at age eleven, when her father introduced her to the game. Strudwick quickly learned the game, and in 1982 she finished fourth in the European Junior Championships. Strudwick eventually played her way on to the European Tour, where she competed for nine years before joining the American tour.

Strudwick's top finishes in 1993 were a tie for fifth place at the Jamie Farr Toledo Classic and a tie for tenth in the Standard Register Ping Tournament. She won the Rookie-of-the-Year award with a total of 226 points, nineteen more than her nearest competitor.

SUZANNE STRUDWICK'S FIVE TIPS ON LIFE AND GOLF:
1. Get yourself organized and know what you want to do in life.
2. Set goals and establish directions to get there. Then you have a purpose and a clear understanding of where you want to be and what you want to do.
3. Don't live beyond your means. That is, don't get carried away in whatever you're doing or with what the Joneses are doing. Getting financially in debt is horrendous. Stick to the standards that you can live to, that you're happy with, and are within your means.
4. In golf, you must have your foundations right for your golf swing. Check your center continually when you're practicing. Have your pro come out and ask him for a ten-minute lesson in which he

or she can check your center. This involves the foundation to the golf swing—the set-up, your grip, your stance—everything involved before you take your club away.

5. Play within yourself. If you've got 130 yards and your buddy has just pulled out a nine-iron, don't think that you have to pull out a nine-iron just to keep up. If you have to hit that eight-iron, just hit the eight and swing easy. The same goes with a par-four hole with water in the front. Don't force yourself to try to hit over the water, even if your buddy can. Don't be forced into playing a shot that you're anxious about or don't think you can pull off.

Author's royalties donated to Alternative Ministries

C h a p t e r   F i f t e e n

BERNIE KOSAR
N F L   A L L - P R O   Q U A R T E R B A C K
speaks out on...

HONORING COMMITMENTS:

I've had to prioritize and budget my time trying to get through all the things that go on, not only in my life, but also in off-the-field things such as charities, banquets, and other similar requests. I've been married three years and have two kids, yet it's trying to find that time to spend with my family that has become a little harder. I really am trying to concentrate on being around our kids.

(Former NFL quarterback) Brian Sipe had a great quote when he said, "You know, I've heard people say that parents need to spend quality time with their kids. Actually, quality time is important, but so is quantity time to the point where your kids should be able to get accustomed to having you around, knowing that you're going to be there for them. That is even more important."

Being a family man with so many public responsibilities is one of the most difficult things to do, because you can conceivably be doing something for somebody every day of the year. That's where you really have trouble, because it's hard to say no to people.

Everybody expects you to just say yes to them, and it's very hard because you do want to. I know I've been blessed to be in this position. God has blessed me so much in what I've been given—not only on the field, but also off the field with my family. That's why I feel an obligation to give as much back as I can, yet it's impossible to do every request.

You know, there's only one of me, and sometimes I get days when there are three charity things to do that day—all of them great—and there is time for only one. Whichever one I decide to do, I'm going to disappoint two people. I end up losing in that situation, because even by just doing the one, I'm also going to be away from my family all that day, too. So, it's really hard and that's what I wrestle with now; how exactly do I decide what to do?

I tend to steer a lot of my actions in charities toward the kids. I really think it's tough on kids these days. There are a lot more distractions out there for them growing up, and I want to try to be as good a role model as I can for them.

Our lifestyle has been very hard on our family. I moved into a new house in Florida last February. We had a baby April 30—our second— then moved into a new house in Cleveland in June. A month later, I left for training camp, so I was gone for a month. Then I got released by the Browns midway through the season, and moved the family down to Florida. Two weeks later, after I had signed with the Dallas Cowboys, they moved into a new house in Dallas, and then we moved back to Florida after the season. So, my wife, Babette, has been really busy, moving two kids while moving in and out of homes and trying to keep everybody on a schedule. Plus, there really isn't an off-season now, because I'm a free agent, and besides, the sport has basically become a year-round practice routine.

When you're a Christian like I am, you feel that obligation of wanting to give back to people and the community. I tend to steer a lot of my actions in charities toward the kids. I really think it's tough on kids these days. There are a lot more distractions out there for them growing up, and I want to try to be as good a role model as I can for them. There are so many great causes just within that group. One day recently (February 1994), we had the Bishop's Cup golf tournament for Catholic kids, and the next day there was a tournament to benefit a children's home for abused kids. Taking part in those things is very important to me, because I want to help these kids get the same chances I've been blessed with over the years.

I started out supporting the Special Olympics when I was in college. That was over a decade ago. Once you do one charity event and get your face around, people see you and you get asked to do more. Recently, I was at a charity event where I was asked to do about six more. I don't feel bad that people ask me, but I feel a little guilty sometimes not being able to honor a lot of those requests. I end up doing probably more than I should because I want to be able to help out people, and I feel good about what I've done in terms of helping people. At the same time, I've tried to shy away from the publicity side of it, because I certainly don't do these things for the sake of exposure. I do it more because I have my own foundation in Cleveland. I have my own charity golf tournament, and I see the good money that can be raised and the good that can be done. I just juggle my time commitments as best I can, always keeping my family at the forefront.

I grew up in a really good, close, Catholic family. I have a sister a year younger and a brother four years younger. My parents have always been there for all three of us, even to the point where you know that their own personal life, while I wouldn't say it suffered, was geared toward their three kids. That really showed me something about sacrifice. They gave up a lot so the rest of us could get the most possible out of life.

We went to church every Sunday together and spoke openly of religion. I went to Catholic school for first grade through eighth grade. We were always around doing things together as a family. When I was a junior in high school, my dad was working for U.S. Steel. That's when the steel industry was going terribly in the northeast. He was going to get transferred to Dallas. But because I had a chance to start and play football at the high school I was going to, he wouldn't move the family. He didn't think it would be good for me to have to start over in another high school and give up that chance of possibly quarterbacking that team.

At that age, and at that time, that was a really huge thing for him to do—to give up a sure job, just so his son could have an opportunity to play quarterback, not knowing at that point that I had any potential to be a good college quarterback or professional quarterback. That really showed the kind of commitment he had toward us and what he thought of his family, because he put us first in everything. My parents are still my best friends.

Being a Good Role Model:

There's an underlying tone of cynicism in our society that's a little more prevalent now, or maybe I'm just older and I recognize it now. At times, our society is a very materialistic one—a what's-in-it-for-me society. Not all people really believe that; and I try not to fall into that trap, although I believe we all have at least a little of that inside us. That comes out in your personality when you're out doing the different events or just when you're on the street meeting people.

I run into so many kids, and even if I'm busy, tired, or have something to do, I really try to acknowledge them in a positive way. When I see a little kid, adolescent, or teenager, I remember back to when I was that age. If I met a pro athlete then—even if it was just for ten seconds—I would remember that my whole life. I want to really make sure that even if it's just a twenty-second conversation I have with somebody, that I'm legitimately nice and talking directly to them; because I know they're going to remember it

I really like to talk to kids. A lot of kids want to talk to me about football and about being a professional quarterback. As quickly as I can, I turn the topic of conversation to what they're doing in school and how their classwork is coming. Like I said, God has blessed me to have the opportunity to be a pro football player. I've played nine years. The average career for an NFL guy now is about three-and-a-half years. Furthermore, you've got to be so, so fortunate to get to this level in the first place. But even if you do, with the average career length being what it is, you're looking at being twenty-five years old and facing a new career.

If you don't have your high school diploma or your college degree—something educationally to fall back on—you don't have a chance. You have the majority of your life to live as a nonathlete. I'm thirty, and while I'm young in the eyes of society in general, I'm old in terms of football. You have to have that education to fall back on, and I really try to get that point across when I'm talking to kids, groups, or just meeting people.

Television shows, such as those with Bart Simpson, and Beavis and Butthead, are more adult-types of humor that I'm not sure are so good for younger kids. That stuff formulates personalities and determines the way some kids react. It's a little tougher growing up these days because there are a lot of things out there that make it harder on kids.

People have called me a good leader and a good role model, and I'm thankful for that. On the football field, I try to lead by example. I think that carries over to leading by example off the field, by doing the right things, by giving of yourself in the community, by putting stuff back into and not just taking. People see how you give things back and learn a lot about you just by how you treat people. Sometimes, some people get too caught up in their status. As for myself, I haven't always been comfortable with all the publicity and focus that comes along with being a professional quarterback.

> **If you don't have your high school diploma or your college degree— something educationally to fall back on—you don't have a chance.**

✳

BERNIE KOSAR

Quarterback Bernie Kosar has never done things by the book during his career in the National Football League.

With his odd, open-legged way of receiving the snap to his side-arm delivery when he throws the football, Kosar has looked a little awkward during his career. But just because Kosar's playing techniques weren't always by the book, it doesn't mean he didn't get the job done.

Heading into the 1994 season, Kosar had thrown for more than 21,000 yards, and connected on 115 touchdown passes. While Kosar's statistics are impressive, one thing stands out in his NFL career: Kosar leads his teams to victory. He quarterbacked the Cleveland Browns to the playoffs five times and reached the AFC Championship Game three times.

In 1994, Kosar reached the Super Bowl with the Dallas Cowboys. He signed with "America's Team" as a free agent after being surprisingly cut by the Browns. Kosar played a major role in getting the Cowboys to the Super Bowl, coming off the bench when Dallas star quarterback Troy Aikman was knocked out of the NFC Championship Game.

Despite coming into the game cold, Kosar completed five of nine passes for 83 yards and an insurance touchdown that sealed the Cowboys' 38-21 victory over the San Francisco 49ers. One week later, Kosar had his first Super Bowl ring as the Cowboys beat the Buffalo Bills 30-13. In April, he signed with the Miami Dolphins.

Kosar's college career at the University of Miami (Florida) was filled with triumphs. Kosar led the Hurricanes to the national championship in 1983 as a redshirt freshman. In Miami's 31-30 Orange Bowl victory over No. 1 Nebraska, he threw for three hundred yards. In 1984, he led the Hurricanes to the Fiesta Bowl. Miami was 19-6 when Kosar started at quarterback.

Kosar and his wife Babette have two daughters, Sara and Rachel. He dedicates a lot of his free time to several charities. His other interests include golf, watching hockey, and studying the stock market.

BERNIE KOSAR'S FIVE TIPS ON LIFE AND FOOTBALL:

1. Lead by example. If you're showing you're willing to work and do things the right way, it rubs off on other people as they look up to you. It says in the Bible to "Do unto others as you would have them do unto you." I think, because of my position and what I've been blessed with, I even have to go beyond that sometimes to treat people even better than sometimes I would expect them to treat me.

2. Get a good education. Some people spend more time thinking about football than they do academics, when academics will carry you a lot longer through life.
3. Don't get too caught up in yourself. I don't get overly serious with myself, thinking I'm someone special. I like to think of myself as just one of the guys. Have a genuine sense of humility.
4. In football, the mental approach is more important than your physical gifts. Work hard to get ahead, even if it means studying plays at night.
5. If you're the quarterback, you're in charge out there.

Author's royalties donated to the Bernie Kosar Foundation

Chapter   Sixteen

LAKE SPEED

W O R L D   C H A M P I O N   A U T O   R A C E R
speaks out on…

FACING DANGER IN PURSUIT OF GOALS:

I can't speak for other race-car drivers, but I've been driving for thirty-three years now, ever since I was thirteen years old. Danger has never really been an issue with me—not that I am a daredevil. I'm not a risk taker, or one who likes to walk on the edge of cliffs. But I think confidence is just part of the thing that erases the danger.

I raced a lot of years prior to becoming a Christian, but danger was not ever the issue. It was always the competitiveness. I was trying to do well, and accomplish goals set to try to win the race. After I got involved in Winston Cup races, danger was probably more of an issue. The cars run two hundred miles an hour, whereas before I had been racing karts at about eighty miles an hour. Even then with the kart, it would decelerate so fast when you took your foot off the gas, that if something happened, it would slow down very fast. In 90 percent of the cases, you didn't have to worry about hitting anything really hard. Lots of people took terrible spills and it looked bad, but most times they would get up and walk away. I raced karts for nineteen years and only went to the hospital one time. It was relatively safe.

But when I got in the Winston Cup cars, I saw 3,500-pound cars traveling around the race track at two-hundred-plus miles an hour, bouncing off the concrete and stuff. I realized there was a little bit more liability here and I had better pay a little more attention, maybe use a little bit more thought in how I drive and in how aggressively I would or wouldn't drive. That was about as much thought as I gave it.

In the last few years, we've had some people injured pretty badly and even had a few fatalities this year. But again, for myself, if I didn't feel called by God to do this, then I would probably be concerned. Every time I get strapped in that car and put the seatbelts on, I know I'm doing what's right for me.

I was one of these people who was brought into this world with a silver spoon in his mouth. My father was one of those success stories kind of people, who went from rags to riches and did real well, yet instilled a real hard work ethic in all of his children. We're a goal-oriented family. At an early age, I was always trying to be the best at whatever I did. I got involved in racing at thirteen and excelled at it, because I worked so hard at it. I went from age thirteen to thirty before I finally won the Karting World Championship in 1978. I had won six U.S. National Championships, and now had reached the ultimate goal in karting.

When I decided I really wanted to try to find yet another goal to reach, I decided I would shoot for the most competitive form of racing there was, and my life had just pretty well been run around racing. It had been the focal point of my life until I got saved. After doing a little research, it became very evident to me that the Winston Cup was the toughest, most competitive form of motor racing on the face of this earth. I was fortunate that it happened to be taking place in the United States and not Europe, which was somewhere I didn't really want to go to live.

Through some amazing circumstances that took place—I'm sure the Lord was already working behind the scenes—I wound up going from a kart to a Winston Cup car in one year with nothing in between. I bounced off some walls early on in my career and realized it was really hard. I thought I never would make it the first year, but then there would always be a race or a few races where I would exceed my expectations. The enthusiasm kept me going and kept me shooting for my goal.

In 1983, I found myself leading the Talladaga 500 on live CBS Television one afternoon. Near the end of the race, something started going through my mind as I was firing down a back straightaway at Talladaga at two hundred miles an hour. I said to myself, "What are you going to do if you win here, too?" It kind of came and went. I wound up finishing third and not winning the race, but obviously in my mind I was getting close to the goal of winning on that level, too. My whole life up to then had just been revolving around racing. If I didn't have a goal in racing to go for, the question really did come to my mind, "What would I do? What is life for? What's this all about?"

I had always just kind of put that stuff off and said, "I won't worry about it, until I'm old and I can't do it any more." I guess the reality of it being within reach drove me to start asking a lot of questions about who I am, why I am here, and what is life all about. Again, a little small voice came back to me and said, "If you want to know the truth, the only place you're going to find any truth in this world today is in that Bible. It's the only thing, and that's not by coincidence, Lake." I thought about that more and it made a lot of sense. How could a book be around this long and not have been changed?

> **I thought I never would make it the first year, but then there would always be a race or a few races where I would exceed my expectations. The enthusiasm kept me going and kept me shooting for my goal.**

I chose to pick up the Bible and start reading. The first thing the devil told me was, "You can't believe anything that book says. It contradicts itself, and all that other stuff." But the little voice told me again, "Why don't you dig it out and read it for yourself instead of taking other people's word for it?" So I did. I started reading and became very convicted of my lifestyle and my values, just everything that I had been doing. I was living in sin with the lady who is my wife now, but at the time she was just my girlfriend. I had a lot of things going on in my life that God couldn't smile on. The sad part really was that up until that point in my life, I had called myself a Christian, since I was fifteen years old, and had gone down front and joined the church. Nothing had changed in my heart or my life, but I had joined the church, been baptized, and went through a ritual, with nothing ever really happening. I was thinking I was really saved.

When I started really studying the Bible, I realized I was really deceived. I wasn't really saved. It started really making an impression on me. I was going to have to start changing my ways. That was in May 1983. It took until August 28, 1983, for me to really determine in my mind that I was ready to give it all up and turn it all over to Him, and let the Lord drive my little race car for a while. I just really had made a mess of things, and it was time to let Him have it.

The idea of the Christian being a defeated, beat-up, second-class citizen, galls me.

I know that the Lord is in total control. The Bible promises that I belong to Him and He's got me in His hands. Nobody or nothing in the world can do one thing to me that He doesn't allow them to do. I just claim Romans 8:28 every day, which says that all things work for the good of those who love the Lord. I'm trying to do that to the best of my ability, and it doesn't make any difference what comes. I'm going to try my darndest to find the good in it, whatever it is, because I'm promised that there is good in it, whatever it may be. I just totally trust in Him that way.

At the same time, I know I'm applying myself as hard as I can to be successful in the arena that God has put me in, because I want to be able to hold His banner high and have it be something that I feel would make Him proud and also make others be drawn to Christ. The idea of the Christian being a defeated, beat-up, second-class citizen, galls me. We're the children of the King; it all belongs to us.

Many people have a distorted view of the world of motor sports, thinking it to be a tough life with crummy conditions. But I think any workplace could be looked at that way. It's just the eyes that you behold them through. When you're looking across the fence into an unknown area, everything looks mysterious.

Most people, when they come to look at motor sports, attend an event, or are exposed to it in any way, see it as something new and mysterious, because they don't understand the mechanics of it. They don't understand the workings and goings-on there. The reality of it is that we're human beings just like everybody else. We still deal with the exact same temptations, struggles, and hardships that every other human being does. It's no different.

God created every person for a specific reason, for a specific work. He's got His own way for each one of us. He created Lake Speed to drive a race car, and He gave me the mentality, the makeup that it takes to sit in a car for four hours at speeds surpassing two hundred miles an hour, where it's hotter than blue blazes, and have fun doing it. He did not create me to be taken out of that environment and placed on a baseball field to stand around and watch some dude throw a ball at a guy hitting with a bat all day. I can't do that. He didn't give me the physical attributes to do it. He didn't give me the mental attributes to do it.

I guess what I'm saying, again, is that each one of us has been gifted by God and placed in certain places, and if we seek God's will for our lives, He will show us where He wants us. If we get in that place, we'll be happier than we could be anywhere else. It doesn't matter if it's digging a ditch or driving a race car. If we're there, we'll know it. People will see you and almost have a hard time understanding "how that guy can be so happy when he's got it so bad." A lot of people would say, "I'd be scared to death to drive that car at two hundred miles per hour."

Well, let me tell you something: I am not in love with this world or this life. When I found Jesus and really started reading the Bible, I really believed that heaven is so much better than this, without all the pain and struggle and anxieties and whatever. If He wants to take me home tomorrow, I am ready, because the idea of dying in a race car is not a bad deal. I would hate to leave my wife and kids, and I told them, "You know I don't really want to go, but if I do go, don't grieve for me, grieve for yourselves, because you're the ones that are going to be left back here."

To a nonbeliever, everything in the Bible sounds like foolishness.

So you really have to be born again before you really understand it—before it does make sense. We can't talk somebody into believing in Jesus Christ. That's a gift from Him. The faith to believe is a gift from God. I think all we can do is point people to Christ, and then it's between Christ and them in terms of salvation. During those times I have an opportunity to share my faith, I don't preach. In fact, I don't know the word of God from cover to cover.

All I know is what God did in my life. I do know that program cover to cover, and I don't need any notes to talk to you about it. He changed my life and gave me a reason to live. He's given me hope. He's restored me in many areas. I lost custody of a child to a divorce, and He gave me a new family and gave me back custody of my child. He has just made life wonderful, when it was miserable before. I was living in the old me, with a selfish lifestyle. He showed me that there's a whole lot more happiness and a whole lot more joy in living for other people, instead of living for myself.

When I won the world championship, that was a culmination of nineteen years' worth of racing all over the country, days and nights, all day, all night, losing a wife, and losing custody of a child. All these things are results, but in the end I did get what I was going after. I won the world championship, and there I was standing on the podium amid a big celebration, flowers, and champagne. What hit me fifteen minutes after the celebration started was that there wasn't but one other person there who I knew. You know what it's like to have a big party and only one person shows up? Not good. That was a real reality check.

I guess the Lord has shown me through His word and through His ways that we are all equal in His eyes and everything that we have is a gift. The fame and the fortune that I may or may not have is totally a gift from Him, and He can give it and He can take it away. There is no guarantee that because you've got it today, you'll have it tomorrow.

Everything He's taught us is for us to share and to help those around us, and not be self-centered, but be selfless. The biggest war is in trying to gauge how much of me should I give to the world and those around me, and how much should I save for myself, time-wise, with my family. How much do I go out and do to help others? How much do I stay around the house and spend time with my own children and my wife? There are a lot of people pulling and asking for my time.

�֍

LAKE SPEED

Winston Cup driver Lake Speed's career is on the rise.

After struggling as an independent owner/driver for more than ten years, Speed proved his worth when he was given a chance to compete for a professional team.

In the 1993 season, Speed was pressed into service as the "interim" driver for the Robert Yates team. Once he got an opportunity, he put the pedal to the metal. Speed ran in the top five at Watkins Glen and finished seventh at Michigan, and challenged for the lead at Bristol before he was involved in a wreck.

Once he was an independent again after the season, Speed found many teams bidding for his services for the 1994 season. He chose the Ford Quality Care team and drives with Bud Moore Engineering. Now, Speed should be able to show what he can do when he has the support he needs.

Speed has won more than $2 million in career prize money. He won the 1988 TranSouth 500, has placed among the top five twelve times in his career, and notched sixty-two top-ten finishes.

Before he got into Winston Cup racing, Speed was a very successful kart racer. He is a six-time U.S. National Kart Champion and won the 1978 World Karting Championship in LeMans, France.

Off the track, Speed likes to spend time with wife Ricé and their four children; Chambers, Sara Ann, Maurie, and Christopher.

LAKE SPEED'S FIVE TIPS ON LIFE AND AUTO RACING:
1. Prayer every day is so important. When you pray is also important. Start the day in prayer and ask God to lead you through the day.

2. In whatever you do in dealing with people, put yourself in their shoes before you speak and think how what you're going to say is going to come across.
3. Pray together with your spouse, out loud.
4. Don't try to do what your circumstances won't allow you to do. In auto racing, that means don't try to make the car do something it is incapable of. Go back to the pits and fix it. Don't try to force it.
5. Forgive. Vengeance is the Lord's, regardless of whether you've been cheated or whatever.

Author's royalties donated to Motor Racing Outreach

C h a p t e r   S e v e n t e e n

MIKE GARTNER

N A T I O N A L   H O C K E Y   L E A G U E   S T A R

speaks out on…

STICKING WITH IT:

Perseverance plays an important part in any athlete's life just from the standpoint of having to go through all the necessary steps that it takes to get to a certain level. Then once you get to that level, it takes sticking with it to be able to maintain where you are.

When I played minor hockey in Canada and started to work my way up through the ranks, I experienced firsthand what it meant to stick with it, believing that I could one day become a professional hockey player. As a result, I finally realized that goal and made it to the National Hockey League (NHL). Once you've made it there, the tough part is staying there, considering all the adversity that you have to go through and perseverance that you have to show in order to maintain a certain level of consistency over that period of time. There is no such thing as real job security as a professional athlete, either.

There is a lot to endure trying to make it and then stay there as an NHL player. You have all the aches and pains, all the wins and losses, and all the ups and downs. Again, you just have to play through all that. Over that time, I've developed a philosophy of learning from my mistakes and continuing to plug away. That's one of the reasons that I've been able to play for fifteen years.

Over those fifteen years, I've had a lot of injuries. But they weren't that serious, because I can look back and see where I haven't really missed that many games. I played through a lot of injuries. I got hit in the eye once in the early part of my career, and for a couple weeks I wasn't sure whether or not I was going to regain the sight in that eye. That was a scary time. It was one of those things that presented a strong test of my faith in God.

I got hit in the eye once in the early part of my career, and for a couple weeks I wasn't sure whether or not I was going to regain the sight in that eye. That was a scary time. It was one of those things that presented a strong test of my faith in God.

I've had two knee surgeries. I've had elbow surgery, a couple of other knee injuries, torn cartilage in my ribs, and various numbers of stitches—not to mention all the bumps and bruises, which are things you are expected to play through at this level. You're expected to be on the ice. Most of the time you're not feeling 100 percent. Some little thing might be wrong with you and it's a nagging sort of thing. But we get paid to play through things like that.

Two years ago, we (the New York Rangers) had the best record in the NHL. We finished first overall, had a great season, then went to the second round of the playoffs, where we ran into the Pittsburgh Penguins. We ended up losing to them and they went on to win the Stanley Cup. Last year (1992-93)—with basically the same team—we didn't even make the playoffs.

There were certainly times during that season which were extremely disappointing, realizing that we had a very talented team, but yet we were a classic case of underachievers. It was an embarrassing time and, of course, a difficult time. So I really don't have to go too far back in my past to see the ups and downs that seem to happen on a daily basis in a lot of respects, and certainly from year to year.

I've been a Christian now for thirteen years. I made the decision to commit my life to Jesus Christ during my second year as a professional. Since then, I have found that I can keep myself at a very even keel because of the faith that I have in Christ. Whether it be the highs or the lows, the highs don't seem to get too high, and the lows don't seem to get too low. That's because of my faith, and I realize that God is in complete control of my life. I trust that He is not making any mistakes, whether it be a time where we are winning and things are going very well personally, or whether it be a time that we are losing and things aren't going that well personally. I know that God is in control of those situations, and I have an assurance that I will get through them.

It's always easier, certainly, to get through the good times. You just have to make sure that you don't get too big a head during those times. Don't get too caught up in yourself and the success that you have. I think that the faith that I have allows me to do that. Even in the more difficult times, I know that God has a plan for this. Having faith in God is not getting too down when things aren't going well or the team isn't playing well.

The more I think about it, the proper word for me now isn't really perseverance—it's preservation. I've kept myself in very good physical condition over the years and really don't feel any differently than I did a number of years ago. But it's more difficult to stay in shape. After you turn thirty years old, people look at you as being old—if you're an athlete. I had to deal with that when I turned thirty. The way things are, there seems to be a perception that I'm not going to be able to perform at a very high level because I'm getting old. I've had to deal with that and have to continue to deal with that. Now when I'm in a slump, you hear things such as, "He's losing it," whereas if you're twenty-five years old, it's, "Oh, he's just in a slump." That difference of perception is something I deal with all the time.

Having played fifteen years already, I certainly owe a good portion of that longevity to two things: First, I've taken good care of myself physically—both in season and during the off-season—and second, I lead a good lifestyle. I have a very supportive family. My wife Colleen and our two children, Josh and Natalie, are extremely supportive in what I do. They give me the room I need in order to prepare myself for all the games. Certainly, my faith in God has given me this athletic ability and talent. Every time I go out on the ice, I strive to perform the best that I can.

I certainly owe a good portion of that longevity to two things: First, I've taken good care of myself physically— both in season and during the off-season—and second, I lead a good lifestyle. I have a very supportive family.

Consistency in hockey is important, but consistency in my life as a husband, father, and citizen in the community is even more important. I spend pretty much all my spare time with my family. We do everything together. We have a summer home in Canada, where we're on the lake. We go back there every summer. As soon as the kids get out of school, we take off and spend two to three months up there every summer and, basically, we are together all the time. We fish together; we water ski; we play tennis; and we kind of hang out together. We all enjoy each other's company.

I have a strong relationship with my wife. We were childhood sweethearts, and we probably know each other better than anyone else knows us. We're not only husband and wife, but we are also without question best friends. We share everything. We share all the decisions; and we share all the ups and downs together. We have done this for years. That's the strong foundation that we build on. Our children are obviously very important to us, and we spend a lot of time with them. During that time, we put a lot of strokes into them to help shape them into strong individuals as well, with strong character.

FAMILY LIFE:

It's a challenge in today's society to deal with questions when you're talking about morality, how people should treat one another, and how we should fit into a society that should be striving to be a better society than the one we grew up in. It's very difficult, I think, for young people right now, and it's a very big challenge for parents raising kids in this day and age. My wife and I look at that as a real challenge to raise our kids properly in this environment. With television, for instance, we limit our children to an hour's worth of television each day. We let them pick the shows with our guidance. Things like that have proven to be a very positive thing for our kids, with their having input into that decision as well as being limited by the amount of television they're digesting.

We have encouraged them to read; we've read to them since they were babies, and they both have become avid readers, and have read some great literature and great children's books, as well as some classics. They are turning into well-rounded individuals as well.

As an athlete for so many years, I believe I have had a great experience with sports developing a lot of good character traits and some very positive attributes. Of course, that's what we're trying to do with our children, too. We've exposed them to a number of different sports in which they have participated, and they seem to be enjoying that aspect a lot. Also, we have provided them piano lessons while trying to gear them toward being as well-rounded as they possibly can be.

But it is a challenge, and they seem to be bombarded with other influences—not only through television, but through school and their peers. We are not opposed to trying to help direct our children toward certain friends as well. We think that the friends they have play an important part in their lives. They seem to be able to pick very good friends, and we are very pleased with that.

MIXING CHRISTIAN VALUES WITH A ROUGH SPORT:

I don't find a contradiction with this, because that's all I've known my whole life. I've played hockey since I was three years old. To me it's a game—a game I love to play. It can be a very physical game at times. I try to play hard and within the rules of the game (as often as I can). Obviously, I can't do that all the time, but I try to be as physical as I can, because it is a physical sport and it's also an aggressive sport. To me, it's just an extension of the faith that I have.

However, hockey as a whole is years behind other major sports as far as any type of spiritual awakening. The sport has made a lot of strides recently, with a lot of stereotypes broken down over the last few years. There are organizations, such as Hockey Ministries International and the Fellowship of Christian Athletes, that are trying to break down these barriers through hockey schools and through exposing the gospel to kids when they are much younger. Still, I know of only about twenty-five Christian athletes out of the hundreds of players in the NHL.

✳

MIKE GARTNER

Hockey player Mike Gartner, who started the 1993-94 season with the New York Rangers and ended it with the Toronto Maple Leafs after being traded, has always been an offensive force during his illustrious, fifteen-year NHL career.

As Gartner neared the end of the 1993-94 season, he was on the verge of extending his NHL record of consecutive seasons with thirty or more goals to fifteen. Certainly, Gartner has been one of the league's most prolific scorers and proved that when he reached a milestone in 1993. Gartner—while still with the Rangers—scored his 600th career goal against the New Jersey Devils. After he scored the goal, Gartner's stick and puck were sent to the NHL Hall of Fame.

Gartner's career is full of achievements. Entering the 1993-94 season, Gartner had scored more than 1,100 career points (assists and goals). A little past the midpoint of the 1993-94 season, Gartner moved into fifth place on the NHL's all-time list of goal scorers, trailing only Wayne Gretzky, Gordie Howe, Marcel Dionne, and Phil Esposito. A veteran of numerous NHL All-Star Games as well, Gartner scored four goals in the 1993-94 All-Star Game, and was chosen the game's Most Valuable Player.

Durability also is a Gartner trademark. He has played in every regular season game six times in his career and has missed an average of only three games a season.

Gartner's most productive season was in 1985, while playing for the Washington Capitals. He scored fifty goals and totaled 102 points, placing him among the league's top ten scorers that season.

Mike and his wife Colleen have two children, Josh and Natalie, and are involved in several charities. Some of Gartner's off-season hobbies include golf, softball, and tennis.

MIKE GARTNER'S FIVE TIPS ON LIFE AND HOCKEY:
1. Integrity is the foundation of a strong man.
2. Strive for consistency.
3. Success means nothing unless you have family to share it with.
4. Athletes are role models, either good or bad.
5. Have faith through Jesus Christ.

Author's royalties donated to Hockey Ministries International

T R U E
CHAMPIONS

Chapter   Eighteen

SHERYL SWOOPES

N C A A   B A S K E T B A L L   S T A R

speaks out on...

SETTING GOALS AND
SELF-DISCIPLINE:

Back when I was a lot younger and started playing sports, I really didn't know what hard work was, and I didn't have any goals at the time, either. It wasn't until my senior year in high school that I really started to realize what I wanted to do with my life and what hard work it would mean getting those things done.

People had doubts about what I could do because I grew up in a single-parent household. To be where I am today would be sort of like a fantasy thing for me thinking back about it. Back when I was in high school, a lot of my friends were actually giving birth to kids even before they got out of high school, and I'm sure there were some people who thought that the same thing was going to happen with me. At that point, I knew that I didn't want to be like that and had other things that I wanted to do, like going on to college.

When it came time for me to graduate from high school and go to college, my mother was really proud of me. She knew how hard it had been for her to raise a family on her own. I could see the gleam

COURTESY OF TEXAS TECH UNIVERSITY

in her eye. I think my mother knew that it was hard for me because she had seen what was happening with a lot of my friends, and she didn't want that to happen to me.

What really helped was my getting a basketball scholarship, because of my mother being a single mom and working. There was no way I could go to college without such a scholarship. It was really tough too, because I was facing a lot of peer pressure. A lot of it had to do with things like dating, drinking, or just driving around. I knew I couldn't be doing all those things at the same time I was doing my school work and playing basketball.

My first year out of high school— and I'm sure that this is something that really applies to anybody leaving high school and going on to college— I really had to apply myself to what I was doing. That's where self-discipline came in.

It was difficult for me, facing the peer pressure and balancing against what my goals were in college and playing basketball. I wanted to do those things with my friends, but my mother was instrumental in not letting me get off track to go do those things. She could have just said, "Yeah, just go ahead and do it." But I look back now and I'm glad she didn't say that, because it might have changed my whole life.

That's about the time I decided to apply myself to school work and to playing basketball, because I knew that I had a chance to do something there. Even after practice, I would often go back to the gym, either at night or on weekends, to play some more. When I would go back to play, I would always play with guys. That really helped me a lot with my game. Just playing with better competition forced me to do things a lot better. That got me to where I am today, and it certainly prepared me for the level of competition in basketball that I faced playing in college. Guys are a lot more physical than girls are. That really helped me set the foundation for my playing career later in college.

My first year out of high school—and I'm sure that this is something that really applies to anybody leaving high school and going on to college—I really had to apply myself to what I was doing. That's where self-discipline came in. By then, I knew that basketball was my life. But on the other hand, there were still some other things that I had to think about on the side. For one thing, I had to learn how to apply myself studying. If you don't, how else are you going to make your grades and be able to stay eligible for basketball?

I had a new commitment there that I never really had while in high school. I had to learn how to prioritize things better between doing all my school work and all the demands involved with basketball. It was hard my first year out because I was out there on my own. My mother was no longer there to help me with everything. When I was in high school, I couldn't really do that much because my mother was very strict and she kept me from doing a lot of the things that might have gotten me in trouble.

That self-discipline goes back to my family values and the way that my mom raised me. I found myself thinking, "Would this be something that my mother would let me do, or would this be something that she wouldn't want me to do?" There were things that weren't necessarily wrong to do, but I knew that I really shouldn't be doing it anyway. So I just wouldn't do it.

As far as basketball goes, I had to work on everything. I had been a good player in high school. But when you get to junior college, it's a whole different level of play. There are so many things that just go back to the basics of the game, and I wasn't as well-versed in those things as I thought I had been. It was really a learning process for me, and I couldn't afford to be distracted by too many things other than school work.

One of the first things that I noticed about playing junior-college ball was that all the other girls were at least as good as me, if not better. I didn't stand out from the crowd as quickly as I had in high school. I had to work on everything—dribbling, shooting free throws, rebounding, and just learning where to go on the floor for certain plays. It was really tough on me; but it was really good, too, because it forced me to be disciplined in what I was doing. Even today, years later, there are things that I need to be working on all the time. It's just a never-ending process. It really humbles you.

The two things that I definitely want to be working on these days are my ball handling and my defense. I am thankful to God that there are certain parts of my game and certain talents that I have that don't need as much work on as other parts of my game. When I go out there to play, I really commit myself to giving 101 percent all of the time, because I know that's the only way I can do my best. But it can be tough, especially now. I no longer play with a team full time, since I left Texas Tech after my senior season. I don't have a team out there to force me to do better, to work with. I don't have a coach out there pushing me, so it's even harder keeping myself going and working on that, so I just have to commit myself to it. Again, that's where that self-discipline comes in.

Now is a really tough time, too, because I'm doing so much traveling. At the same time, I'm still back in school and it's just so easy for me to get lazy at times. That's when I really have to kick myself to keep myself going. There are times when I just don't feel like working out, but then one of my goals is to play in the Olympics, which are coming up again in 1996, in Atlanta. There's a reason there for me to keep on going and to keep on working on my game, because I'd like to play in the Olympics, which is something that I've never done before. In one respect, I know it's only two years away, but in another way it can seem like forever. That leaves so much time for me to work on staying in tip-top shape.

I am staying in shape the best I can, because in the meantime, we have the World Championships, the Goodwill Games, and the Pan-Am Games coming up. Those give me incentive to keep working on my game. It's so much fun, and yet it's so much hard work that I just need to keep pushing myself. That international experience is really going to help me out a lot, and I'm really looking forward to it.

In truth, I'm a team-sport athlete without a team to play for full time right now. The situation I'm in reminds me of what Michael Jordan said when he retired from basketball. He said something about it not being a challenge to him anymore and that's why he didn't want to play anymore. But for me, it still is a challenge, even after being a part of the ultimate—a national-championship team at Texas Tech. I just love basketball so much and I just want to keep on playing. On top of that, there are so many things that I want to prove to myself, as well as wanting to prove things to other people. That's why I believe I still have a long way to go before I fulfill my career.

The chance to play in the Olympics with other players of that caliber helps keep me going. It's very important as an athlete or in your personal life always to have another set of goals out there. To be honest, there are days when I do get down and do think to myself, "Gee, there really isn't anything to work for; it's just too far off." But it's a day-to-day thing. One thing that keeps me fired up is an Olympic poster from Barcelona (where the 1992 Summer Olympics were held) up on my wall in my room. I like to go to that poster every chance I get and say, "That's going to be me in 1996."

The chance to play in the Olympics with other players of that caliber helps keep me going. It's very important as an athlete or in your personal life always to have another set of goals out there.

It is very frustrating that there isn't a women's league now for me to play in, in the United States. That would certainly help keep me in shape. But then again, as far as self-discipline goes, it's still ultimately up to me how well I can push myself. Only I can do that. I just have to keep on going, keep on working, keep on improving. I have to practice alone, work out alone, go running alone, lift weights alone. I do all those things by myself.

My boyfriend, Eric, is a big help in all this. He's really great; he encourages me day in and day out. He knows that I want to play in the 1996 Olympics and that it's been a goal of mine for a long time. I'm not going to let anything stop me from at least trying to make the Olympic team and playing in the Olympics in 1996.

BEING A TEAM PLAYER:

The main thing with playing with a team that went on to win the national championship was just being on a team of players who really played together, who really liked each other and worked well together. They all accepted their roles really well. Back when I transferred from junior college to Texas Tech, everyone who was already at Tech was really receptive to me and said, "Oh, Sheryl, we're so glad to have you as a teammate." On the other hand, they could have been really cold toward me or whatever, and made it a lot tougher. That type of attitude had a lot to do with why we were so good as a team.

I know that everything I have accomplished, everything I have received up to this point, every honor, every achievement, award or whatever, has been because of my teammates, because of how they helped me and accepted me, and let me fit in so well with them.

The whole thing about it was, they really didn't know what to expect from me; and I certainly didn't know what to expect from them. We were just kind of put in a new situation together and it went very well. I came in my junior year and they allowed me to fit in well. As far as last year goes, our winning the national championship was a team thing; there were no ego problems or jealousy involved.

There were times I became concerned because of all the attention I was getting late in the season. My being singled out could have alienated the other players, but it never came down to that. There could have come a time when they might have said, "Look, Sheryl, we're just tired of this," but that never happened. What was so great about it was that they allowed me to come out in every practice and in every game and do the things that I could do.

I know that everything I have accomplished, everything I have received up to this point, every honor, every achievement, award or whatever, has been because of my teammates, because of how they helped me and accepted me, and let me fit in so well with them. If you're going to play the showoff, you're not being a team player and you're not going to be successful, either as an individual or as a team.

With us at Texas Tech, there were people on the outside saying we didn't have what it takes to win a national championship. What was important was what my teammates were believing and experiencing. You know, everyone might have an individual goal, but if you belong to a team and you strive to make that team your first priority, all of your goals will likely be achieved. So put your team goals ahead of your own individual goals.

DEALING WITH PRESSURE:

In any situation, being under pressure has its advantages and disadvantages. I remember last year getting ready to go to the NCAA Tournament Final Four and my talking to Coach Marsha Sharp. She had me prepared. She told me, "It's going to be wild; it's going to be crazy; and, of course, when you step off the airplane in Atlanta, everyone's going to want to talk to you; and they're going to want to know what you're thinking."

I love having pressure on me, because I want to be in the position to do what I can to help pull the team out of any tight situation. Like if we need a basket, I want people to know, "Hey, we can go to Sheryl and she'll come through for us with a basket." There was a lot of pressure on us last year (during the 1993 NCAA Tournament Final Four) and there was a lot of pressure on me. There was something like sixteen or seventeen thousand people there watching us play. They had heard about me, they had read about me; and I know they expected a lot more out of me. Now that's pressure, and I love that feeling, because it just gives me more determination to go out there and play hard, put up that shot, or go get that rebound.

I know I can't have ten turnovers in a game. I know I'm expected to score twenty-five or more points in a game, and that's a lot of pressure. If I'm out there playing while sick, no one's going to understand if I don't play up to par. No one's going to understand that my being sick might have been a reason for not playing as well. People expect you to play your best at all times.

I love the game so much I just don't look at it as being pressure. In that regard, my faith in God has really helped. I grew up in a church and trusted in the Lord. Although I'm not perfect, I would like to be. I believe my faith in God actually increased over the last couple years at Texas Tech, because I've faced so many situations and met so many people who were new to me. I couldn't deal with it all by myself, and the Lord has always been there for me.

There were times when I could have taken that wrong turn, and God knows where I would be right now. Even today, there isn't a day goes by that I don't pray and thank God for everything. You know there are a lot of people out there who can't believe that I can play sports at this level and still have faith in God. But then I believe without Him, none of this would have been possible—none of what I've accomplished or what our team accomplished could have been done without Him.

A lot of it too goes back to my family values and my mom teaching me right from wrong— what to do and what not to do. Last year before every game, we would all say the Lord's Prayer together, but I would also go off by myself and say my own prayers, too. At the time I thought some of my prayers might have sounded kind of stupid. But they were spoken from the heart. There really is no such thing as a stupid prayer, even if it sounds that way at the time. I know that He's always listening and He's always able to know what I mean by what I pray.

✳

SHERYL SWOOPES

Sheryl Swoopes might be the Michael Jordan of women's basketball.

She achieved this status with her excellent play on the court and her class off the court.

On the basketball court, Swoopes was the star of two great Texas Tech women's basketball teams. During the 1991-92 season, Swoopes averaged almost twenty-two points a game and led the Lady Raiders to the regional finals of the NCAA Tournament.

But it was the 1992-93 season that really established the Lady Red Raiders and Swoopes as national headliners. Swoopes averaged twenty-eight points, nine rebounds, four assists and four blocked shots a game, while leading Texas Tech to its first national championship in women's basketball.

During the 1992-93 NCAA Tournament, Swoopes averaged 35.4 points and nine rebounds a game. Included was a record-setting, forty-seven-point performance in Tech's championship-game victory over Ohio State. It's little wonder that Swoopes won the tournament's Most Valuable Player award.

The list of awards she has won could fill a gymnasium. Swoopes was named the 1993 Associated Press Female Athlete of the Year (the first time the award has been given to a player from a team sport), the 1993 Sudafed Sportswoman of the Year, the Babe Zaharias Award and the 1993 Dunlop Amateur Athlete of the Year (the second female athlete ever to receive it). Of course, this was after she had won about every 1993 college player-of-the-year honor there was.

Swoopes also is a class act off the court. After playing professionally in Italy for a short time in 1993, Swoopes returned to Lubbock to get her degree. She has given speeches, usually to youngsters, in which she has talked about setting goals, working hard, and coping with tough family situations.

SHERYL SWOOPES'S FIVE TIPS ON LIFE AND BASKETBALL:
1. Have faith in God, believing that He will take care of everything.
2. Live life to its fullest every day.
3. Set goals and don't let anything get in your way. Give it 101 percent.
4. Once you become successful, always remember where you came from. Be humble in your accomplishments.
5. In basketball, always stay under control when going to the basket.

Author's royalties distributed among various charities

Chapter   Nineteen

DARRELL WALTRIP

N A S C A R   W I N S T O N   C U P   C H A M P I O N

speaks out on…

COMMITMENT:

I'm real big on commitment. One of the things that young people lack today is a willingness to be totally committed to anything, whether it be the gospel, pursuit of a career, or whatever. There are so many areas where commitment is what it takes to make you successful—to help you get the job done.

I first started learning about true commitment while running track in high school. In track, you have to give up a lot of things to get in shape to run. I was a half-miler and had to run every afternoon. You ran until you threw up. That was how you trained. You could drink Cokes and milkshakes and, in some cases, smoke, but without total commitment, you never really fulfilled your ultimate potential or achieved your ultimate goal. Those who did were the ones who committed themselves to work hard. I was one of those guys.

The first thing I ever found in high school which I could be successful at was being an athlete. I was a fair athlete. I was a fair basketball player. I was a fair baseball player. I was a fair everything, but

I never found anything that I felt as good about as I did running track, so I just committed myself to track. For a couple years in the early 1960s, I was the best half-miler in Kentucky.

Back in those days, a lot of things that are questionable today and a lot of things that kids today argue about weren't open for discussion. Your education was something that was a given. So was your mom and dad staying married, and having a family and eating supper together, going to church together, and all those things that are now the exception. Those were the rules in those days. I think that's one of the things that really has deteriorated in this country. Of course, I'm sure other people echo the same thing and other people say the same thing, but the deterioration of the families is one of the big reasons why this country doesn't have people who are committed like they were twenty years ago.

The thing that bothers me is that I have two young daughters. One is six years old and one is eighteen months old. They are going to grow up in a society that's not anything like what I grew up in. The world as I knew it and the world as it's been in the past is on the verge of being a whole new world that none of us will recognize. That's scary. Like the Bible says, you just train 'em up. Do the best you can do.

We're a Christian family and go to church together. We do everything we can together. Stevie, my wife, and I try to be a good mother and a father, and husband and wife, and set as good an example as we can in front of the children at all times, and hopefully that will have an impact on them as they grow older. As a father, I would like my children to see me as a father who has a career that he pursues with all his heart, but they also see a father who loves them and makes every effort to include them in what he does. That's the big thing for our family. We try to do everything that we possibly can as a family, together.

Commitment also means a lot to me in terms of overcoming adversity. In July 1990 at Daytona, I was in a bad crash. I shattered my left leg, broke my left arm and had a serious concussion. I was in pretty bad shape for quite a while. That was the first time I had ever been injured—it was the first time that I'd ever had to miss racing because of an injury in a race car.

After I started to get well and heal up, I started a rehab program. Now, I'm talking about a guy in his forties. In fact, I was forty-three years old and felt I had had a very successful career. It was pretty tough to make the commitment to rehabilitate myself to the point where I could make myself get back out there and race again and be competitive again. It took a lot of heart, soul, guts, sweat and tears to get back into condition where I could get back into a race car and race again. But I did that in two months. It was pure hell.

> It was pretty tough to make the commitment to rehabilitate myself to the point where I could make myself get back out there and race again and be competitive again. It took a lot of heart, soul, guts, sweat and tears to get back into condition where I could get back into a race car and race again.

I went to rehab five days a week and worked with my upper body to get my upper body strong, while my leg healed. When my leg got strong enough for me to start working with it, I rode an Aerodyne stationary bike every day for five days a week with one leg. Those are the types of things I did to rehab my leg. I made a miraculous recovery from the injury I had and was back in competition.

The first time I got back into a car, I came in third in a race in Richmond, Virginia. It was the worst of times and yet it was the best of times. Through it all I never questioned the Lord. I never asked, "Why did this happen to me?" I knew it happened to me for a reason, and one of the big reasons was that it showed me that I needed to be in a physical-fitness program. I started working out on a regular basis after my rehab. All this actually made me a better race-car driver. I realized that as I had gotten older, it had gotten harder and harder for me to run three-and-a-half or four-hour races. It was almost like I was a kid again. Still, it wasn't something I would have chosen.

Commitment also has meaning in everyday family life. My wife and I didn't have children for eighteen years, because we had three miscarriages in that time. We were just about to accept the fact that it wasn't meant for us to have children of our own—although we continued trying many things. My wife's mother had taken the drug DES back in the days when they didn't know how much harm it did to the child. In Stevie's case, it damaged her reproductive organs. It was something we couldn't do anything about, although she had had a couple of surgeries to try to improve that. We were kind of getting down to the last straw, because I was fixing to turn forty, and at that age it's very difficult to adopt.

We were right on the verge of adopting a child when Stevie got pregnant. We just felt that it was the Lord at work, because she wasn't even supposed to get pregnant. We kind of waited to see what was going to happen; and she had Jessica, and she was beautiful. That was our first child. We had her when I was forty-two and Stevie was thirty-seven. They told us not to worry because we would never have another one. But four years later, we had another one. The Lord blessed us in our commitment to having our own family, and we never gave up. We knew that in the Lord's time, He would give us a child if it was meant to be.

> **Commitment to me goes a lot further back in a person's life, to the beginning. After that, it becomes discipline and respect and all the things that we were taught as children growing up.**

Commitment in faith is tested daily. Being a Christian living in today's society is probably not a very popular role to be in. But it's just one of those things that I believe in and I believe in the Lord. I believe in God, I believe in our country, and I believe that some day this country will see the light and go back to its traditional values. When we do that, I'll be right at home.

It's pretty obvious that you're either committed to something or you're not. In most cases, people are just involved. Commitment to me goes a lot further back in a person's life, to the beginning. After that, it becomes discipline and respect and all the things that we were taught as children growing up. Respect your elders, and obey the authorities and the law. Those are not anything new. They're just traditional values, and nobody wants to hear that anymore. It's something that kids today don't hear enough of, and I think it's something that we could do a lot better job of.

The first thing you do is honor your mother and father. That's just very basic. The next thing is, you can pray and respect the Lord. Know who the Lord is and have a relationship with the Lord. Have respect for other's property and valuables. Value other people's opinions. The biggest thing wrong with our society today is that we live in a "blame" society. We want to blame all our problems on someone else. Children today want to blame what's wrong with them on their parents, because their parents didn't bring them up properly, abused them, or whatever. Young people today have too many options, and they always want to blame everything that happens to them or why they are the way they are on someone else, when actually it's their own responsibility.

STRESS:

One of the worst things of all is trying to be all things to all people. Trying to be a good dad, trying to be a good husband, trying to be a good Christian, trying to be a good race-car driver, trying to be a good team owner, trying to be a good ambassador for my sport, trying to be so many things—it's tough. You become very frustrated when you find yourself in that situation of trying to be a leader in everything that you do. That, to me, is natural with the way I am. I want to be the leader; I don't want to be the follower. But it becomes very frustrating at times.

That frustration is where the stress comes from. So you just have to sometimes sit down and prioritize what's important: What can I do in this situation? What can I do in that situation? You might know in your heart you are doing the best you can...the best you know how. That's how I handle stress.

A lot of times I just sit down and talk to the Lord and say, "Lord, help me and give me the patience and understanding I need in these situations to do the best that I can do." The most common thing I can do is to spend a few minutes by myself—quiet time, if you will—and get my thoughts together, and know that I'm doing things in the right priority.

✳

DARRELL WALTRIP

Darrell Waltrip is one of auto racing's legends. The NASCAR Winston Cup driver has accomplished things in racing most people only dream about. He has won NASCAR's biggest award, the NASCAR Winston Cup championship, three times in his career. This award is given annually to the driver who accumulates the most points in a season. Heading into the 1994 season, Waltrip was the all-time leading active NASCAR Winston Cup winner with eighty-four victories. He also has finished in the top five in races 266 times and has more than 360 top-ten finishes in his career. In financial terms, Waltrip's success translates to more than $12.5 million in prize money. And Waltrip has won just about every NASCAR Winston Cup race there is, ranging from the small to the major races—the four NASCAR Winston Cup Select Million Dollar Events (Daytona 500, the Coca Cola 600, the Mountain Dew Southern 500 and the Winston Select 500). His last major victory was the 1992 Southern 500, where he won more than $76,000 in prize money. Waltrip's success continued in the 1993 season, when he won more than $650,000 in prize money, had ten top-ten finishes and tied for thirteenth in the final season standings.

Waltrip and his wife Stevie have two girls; Jessica Leigh and Sarah.

DARRELL WALTRIP'S THREE TIPS ON LIFE AND AUTO RACING:
1. One of the biggest things for me, that I tell my crew, and I try to tell myself all the time, is don't beat yourself. That's one of the hardest lessons to learn and it's one of the easiest things to do. You get so concerned about where you are and what you're doing that when you make a mistake, you beat yourself.
2. Don't make the same mistake twice. I like to say, "Don't get bitten by the same dog twice." That's one of the rules that we have here.
3. You can get a lot more out of a mule patting him on the back than kicking him in the hiney.

Author's royalties donated to Motor Racing Outreach

C h a p t e r   T w e n t y

BOBBY BOWDEN

N C A A C H A M P I O N S ' F O O T B A L L C O A C H
speaks out on...

LEADERSHIP:

The biggest way in which my style of leadership has changed over the years—and I'm talking about forty-one years of coaching—is that I live my life more Christian-patterned than it was when I got started in this. At least, I hope I have grown in my Christian life through the years.

I've tried to be a better example to my players. I've tried to lead by my own life, because I've always felt that actions speak louder than words. To say one thing and do something else tears down everything that you say.

At Florida State, we start every coaching-staff meeting with a devotion and a prayer, where each coach is assigned a certain day to take the lead. This is not done as some sort of good-luck charm, either. I do it because I want to do it, and I feel like it's good for all of us. There are usually about seventeen of us in our staff meetings, counting the trainers, managers, assistant coaches, graduate assistant, head coach, etc. That means every seventeenth day my number comes up. We've been doing that for a long time just as a way of looking for guidance and direction. That's probably as good a thing as we do. I think it's very important.

A lot of times when I make speeches to organizations, I recommend to them that they do the same thing. Seek guidance in the decisions you have to make. I think it's harder to make bold decisions that are righteous, because of the way society has changed. There's just more open room for people who don't believe, don't have a faith, and/or are trying to hinder your ministry to step in and push things off track. Separation of church and state has always been an issue, and it can be carried overboard either way, I'm sure. Although there would be objections to any type of religious affiliations you might try to have with your ball club, we do recommend the Fellowship of Christian Athletes to our student-athletes here. We have a chapter on our campus and quite a few boys participate in it. We also encourage them to try to get the other kids involved.

The idea of leadership is important among the players as well as the coaches. I think it helps if you recruit individuals who are leaders. Like anything else, of course, it's a lot better if you've already got them—natural leaders. When we recruit players, we look for young men with character. Then when they get here, we try to encourage them to set an example. Peer pressure is the strongest pressure you can get in this world. If your peers are doing it, it's much easier for you to do it. So we do try to pinpoint leaders on our football team and get them to take an active part in trying to get the other boys to follow.

The negative influences against bold, righteous leadership are stronger than they have ever been. Much of that is because so many of the fathers—as well as some mothers— have become negligent in setting examples for their children. Fathers, especially, need to be stepping up and doing a better job of showing children the right way to go. The best form of leadership as a parent is raising children in a Christian home, going with them to church, and teaching them the Bible and how to pray. But as it stands now, those are things that are lacking.

The thing that is weakening our nation more than anything is the tearing down of the family. It's just so obvious with the children on the streets now carrying guns, staying out late, or causing problems, that they have no direction from home. It's a big breakdown we have in our society.

As leaders, it is one of our responsibilities to get the right message out. For a lot of us coaches, there's a personal calling in that regard. I feel strongly that I have an obligation to get out and speak. Football gets people's attention. However, football is not the priority of my life; it's just a priority. The priority is my faith in Jesus Christ and trying to serve God to the best of my ability, which is why I think everybody was put here on earth in the first place.

Everybody is hungry for that word. The problem is, we don't have enough people to go out and stand up for it. With some of the groups I talk to, it can get pretty amazing. I had an interesting thing happen a few years ago, when I spoke at a stag party in a major city. I won't mention the city or group to save them embarrassment; but when I say stag, I simply mean it was all men in that group.

I was the featured speaker, and it was a big-deal type of event, with some star players there. As it turned out, it was the most vain banquet I had attended in years. By that, I mean it was a place where God's name was continually taken in vain. Dirty, filthy jokes were told throughout. It seemed like the nastier they would get, the more fun they were having.

In my opinion, our standard of living keeps going up in this country while the standard of life keeps going down. The thing that's killing us is television.

Well, while sitting there listening to all this, I was determined that when it was my turn to speak, I would make them laugh more than all those other guys telling the filthy stuff. I would tell them clean stories and clean jokes. When I finally got up to the podium, I started off by telling them that on the previous day, I had spoken in a church down in Alabama. I did that just to let them know from the start where I was coming from. I ended up getting as good applause and more laughs than those guys who were so filthy. What I'm saying is, I think people are hungry for it. There are just not enough people presenting the message to them, that's all.

In my opinion, our standard of living keeps going up in this country while the standard of life keeps going down. The thing that's killing us is television. Television is nothing but killing, rape, stealing, crime, and undisciplined life. The kids are seeing it day after day, hour after hour, if their parents let them. A lot of the parents aren't with their kids while the TV is on. They don't know what their kids are seeing, and what they're seeing is painting pictures inside the minds of these kids.

I was always taught that things entering your mind eventually have to come out in one form or another. A lot of our crime is out there because kids see how easy it is to kill. Kids are seeing how easy it is to rape. Kids are seeing how easy it is to steal. They are seeing all this on television—daily, daily, daily. That's something that's really killing us, and unless the people who are responsible for these programs become more moralistic, it's likely to take us down as a society. I sometimes catch myself sitting there, having watched television for three hours, thinking, Hey, all I'm watching is trash.

By today's standards, even what we call a good program has some garbage in it. One main thing to consider: Are you spending equal time listening to God? Are you spending equal time reading your Bible? Are you spending equal time going to Sunday school and going to church? Why not? I'm just afraid the formula is getting way out of whack in that regard.

There are times I question myself in terms of leadership, and while I don't think it should be this way, I think it really only affects me when I lose. I question myself, "Am I doing the right thing? Am I strong enough? Am I doing everything that I should do?" That old fear can come sneaking back in on you when you lose. To be honest with you, the more I win the more confident I get and the stronger I make my devotions. It shouldn't be that way, but for some reason it builds my confidence when I speak to kids about it.

I love to speak to churches, get involved in the FCA (Fellowship of Christian Athletes), and want to be on Billy Graham's program and the "700 Club." There's a reason for this. It goes back to when I was a kid in high school. One day, we had an All-American come to my church and give his testimony. My being a football player, I was sitting back in the back row, where I usually never paid attention the way I should. But boy, I wanted to hear this guy, because he was an All-American.

He changed my life. His name was Jackie Robinson, and he used to be a basketball player at Baylor University. He spoke about when he was a college student. That meant so much to me—getting to listen to an All-American. That's one reason I feel that if nobody else can, I can attract young men to listen to my message, because I know first-hand that young players out there will look up to a coach and look up to All-Americans. I have an obligation to talk to those kids every chance I get.

Anytime I hire a new coach or a young coach, the first thing I tell him is, "Look, you're not one of the guys anymore. You're now one of the coaches, and we need you to be a role model for these young men." What's happening is this: Many of these kids don't have fathers. Take my football team here at Florida State. I don't know the exact number, but I wouldn't be surprised if 45 to 50 percent of these players did not have a man in their house back home. We coaches have a great opportunity to fulfill this fatherly role to the best of our abilities.

What I'm saying is that teachers and coaches are now having to take the place of fathers and, in many cases, even the mothers. Therefore, we have a great opportunity to help.

I try to keep that in the back of my mind as I work with these young men. In fact, I tell them, "When you come to Florida State, I am now your daddy—well, in my case maybe your granddaddy. Even if you've got a daddy at home, he can't be up here with you, so I want y'all to use me. Come in here and see me if you've got a problem. I'll keep it quiet—just you and me, and we'll discuss it." A lot of times kids will come to me; a lot of them won't. I wish they all would, because I think I could help them. Those who do come in usually have a problem that's big to them. But with my experience and my age, I know what they're going through, because maybe I went through something like it and can help them.

What I'm saying is that teachers and coaches are now having to take the place of fathers and, in many cases, even the mothers.

Therefore, we have a great opportunity to help. Maybe we can pull these kids out of the direction they are going by substituting for the lack of parenthood at home.

I've always felt that when that day comes, and we all die and we go before God and His judgment, and even though we Christians believe we are saved through His grace, we still are going to be judged. I think that the worst thing that can happen to us through judgment is for God to say, "Yeah, but you caused so-and-so to go to hell, or you caused so-and-so to fail, or you caused so-and-so to go the wrong way." That's the responsibility I do not want to get nailed for—my causing another guy to go down. That's scary.

As I've gotten older, I've done better in that regard. Back in my early coaching days, my thoughts were where they are with a lot of coaches—win, win, win at any expense. The feeling was that you had to win—well, actually you do have to win—or they will fire you. But you don't have to cheat, and you don't have to beat up and exploit kids for this to happen. That's a responsibility we have today in the coaching profession.

✳

BOBBY BOWDEN

Veteran and popular college football coach Bobby Bowden finally won the big one in 1993.

After his Florida State Seminoles football teams finished second in the nation's final rankings several times in the late 1980s and early 1990s, Bowden led the Seminoles to their first national championship in 1993, as Florida State defeated Nebraska, 18-16, on New Years' Day 1994 in the Federal Express Orange Bowl.

For Bowden, it was a long road getting there. Bowden arrived in Tallahassee in 1976 and helped build the Florida State program into a national powerhouse. By 1980, the Seminoles were a team to be reckoned with as they played in two consecutive Orange Bowls.

The 1980s brought more success to Bowden and Florida State. The Seminoles won an average of about nine games a year and played in a bowl game every year during the decade. During the 1980s, FSU posted an 8-1-1 record in post-season bowl play. But with all the success of the 1980s, and continuing into the early 1990s, Bowden and Florida State went through the frustration year after year of having one of the best teams in the nation, only never to win the national title.

Losses to in-state rival Miami killed the Seminoles' title hopes several times. But the 1993 season ended all the FSU frustration. Losing only to Notre Dame, the Seminoles bounced back late in the season for an impressive season-ending victory over powerhouse Florida, before beating Nebraska in the Orange Bowl. The result was Bowden's long-awaited national championship.

Bowden enters the 1994 season with 239 career victories and a .751 winning percentage. Ironically, Bobby wasn't the only Bowden to stake at least a partial claim to the nation's top spot in 1993. His son Terry, in his first year as a Division I head coach, led the Auburn Tigers to a perfect 11-0 regular season, although the Tigers were ineligible for post-season play because of an NCAA probation. Bobby Bowden's two other sons, Tommy and Jeff, are assistant coaches.

Bowden has been married to wife Ann more than forty years. Among his many other off-field interests is studying World War II history.

BOBBY BOWDEN'S FIVE TIPS ON LIFE AND FOOTBALL:

1. Start each day with a systematic Bible study and prayer. By yourself, read Scripture. Do it systematically; don't just pick it up and turn randomly to a page. It could be you start from the front cover and read through to the back. I always say go to the New Testament and start with John. After you do that, read Matthew, Mark and Luke, then go back to the Old Testament and read how everything has happened. Again, start each day with prayer and a Bible study to get your life started off the right way. Seek God's guidance.

2. Remind yourself every day that God is in control. I don't care how bad a situation you are in, it'll end. On the other hand, I don't care how good things are going, it's not going to last.

3. Unless you have problems, you either have a very boring life or are probably at the cemetery. It's the solving of these problems that

builds character. You can't build character unless you can overcome problems.

4. In football, play one down at a time. Don't try to look ahead and say "Ahhh, I've got sixty minutes left and I'm going to be so tired; oh, I'm going to get beat up." Play it one play at a time, as hard as you can.

5. Before you play the game or practice, ask God to help you to do your best.

Author's royalties donated to Fellowship of Christian Athletes

T R U E
CHAMPIONS

Chapter Twenty-one

RUSSELL MARYLAND

N F L   F O O T B A L L   S T A R
speaks out on...

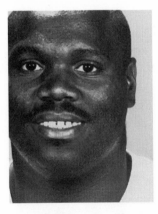

GROWING UP AS A YOUTH:

When I was growing up, we had the same situation with drugs and crime that we have today. The big problem when I was growing up was gangs. There were some big gangs around there (Chicago) and they had a big influence on the kids. Those kids who felt that they didn't have any parental backing would go and search for the big gangs. That was the big thing in Chicago. Luckily, I had good parents and I stayed away from those gangs.

Right now, kids, more than ever, have gangs to deal with. Another big thing is drugs. Kids today just have to steer clear of those things. The thing that makes drugs so lethal is that kids—especially in areas that are less socioeconomically advantaged—believe the only way out is through money, and society puts so much emphasis on it. There's nothing wrong with having money. But kids go out and try to find an easy way to make money—quick and easy money—so they turn to drug sales and use.

If I was back in Chicago trying to relate to those kids, I would first try to get on their level. I came from similar circumstances. The way you steer clear of drugs and all that type of mess is you find strength in your family, even if it's hard to find. If your parents love you and you know that, you won't try to look for something else as a substitute for that. Obviously, this is as much a message for parents as it is for the kids.

I noticed at a young age that while I wanted to be accepted by my peer group, I realized that my friends weren't going to help me get through school. My friends weren't going to help me be who I was going to be.

I noticed at a young age that while I wanted to be accepted by my peer group, I realized that my friends weren't going to help me get through school. My friends weren't going to help me be who I was going to be. That, coupled with the fact that my parents instilled religious values in me, made me go to church and made me realize that the real teacher is Jesus Christ. That's what saved me. I knew that the only being you can really trust and who won't lead you wrong is God. That's how I got away from the peer pressure.

Gangs are a substitute for the family. I had a strong family upbringing. I had a strong father figure in the home and didn't have to look for a father-figure substitute in some guy out on the street telling me that he was going to be there if I needed help. It all boils down to the structure of the family. I think that's why you get a lot more gang activity, because the structure of the family is breaking down so bad. The thing that I remember from growing up is my father leaving home early in the morning to go to work and not getting home until late. My mother also works. My grandmother and grandfather took care of us between the time we got back from school and the time my mother came and picked us up.

My parents are hard workers. That taught me as I got older that you have to work hard in order to do well and get ahead. As I got older, I also realized that with my parents working so hard, it would be a shame if I let them down by messing it up with drugs, gangs, crime, whatever.

This is where I can help other youths as a role model, getting out to them and telling them how they can find ways not to fall into that mess of gangs and drugs. But a lot of guys who are professional athletes don't feel the need to take that responsibility, because it's too much of a burden to bear. Sure, it's a big responsibility. You're a spokesperson for what is right, but a lot of guys think, Hey, I'm just an average person. I'm not a role model, and I don't want to be a role model. Parents should be the primary role model.

But I think since you are thrust in the position, and can look at how God has been so good to you and put you in that position, you do have a type of moral obligation to go back into the schools and churches, and do those things to let everybody know that this is what God will do for them.

When I was a kid, I used to go to Sunday school every Sunday morning. My parents didn't pressure me to join the church, but they did tell me that when it's your time and the Spirit moves you, you will want to join the church and accept Jesus Christ as your personal Savior. I did that ten years ago, on January 1, 1984. I think I got baptized a couple weeks later and can remember that very well.

I always tell a story about my pastor, Reverend William A. (Augustus) Johnson, back in Chicago. Reverend Johnson is still at the same church, where he's been the pastor for the past fifty-four years. He's ninety-four years old and still going strong. Well, back when I was baptized in 1984, I can remember Reverend Johnson—I was pretty big; about 284 pounds, and he was eighty-four years old at the time—saying, "I'm going to dip you back in this water and you're going to have to find your own way to get back up." So I just planted a foot back there and helped him. I bet that congregation was saying, "Ah man, he's really got the power behind him."

As for the influences on youths today, a lot of it goes back to what is being put on television and radio. Looking at and listening to

As for the influences on youths today, a lot of it goes back to what is being put on television and radio. Looking at and listening to what some of these artists put out, you know that it's got to be tough for kids to decide what's the right message.

what some of these artists put out, you know that it's got to be tough for kids to decide what's the right message. You've got somebody you hear every hour on the radio saying, "I'm going to shoot you, I'm going to do this to your momma and your daughter," and that kind of stuff. You hear that junk so often, but the thing many youths don't hear is what is said in church every Sunday.

The way the mass media presents things has a lot to do with the society we live in. The media is putting things out that children shouldn't be exposed to. Adults can be exposed to that kind of stuff. But most kids don't have the maturity to decipher that that's not the person they want to be. Yet, programmers still play it over the radio and television. As long as the record companies make a profit putting that stuff out, and as long as the television corporations and radio corporations are going to allow that stuff to be played, our kids will be steered the wrong way. It's all about making that money at the expense of any moral obligation.

When I go out and speak to groups of children, I tell them three things: "Obey God, obey your parents, and obey your teachers." I put it in this order, because I tell them without God you wouldn't be here, and your parents wouldn't be here. I tell them, "Don't worry about what your friends think of you. Just worry about doing the right thing and doing what God has planned for you. Everybody in the world can be against you, but as long as God is with you, then you have no problem." Next, I tell them, "Obey your parents. Your parents are experienced people. They brought you into this world and created a life for you. Those are the people that you should get advice from. They make it so that you are able to go to school each day and just all-around take care of you, and they don't want to see anything bad happen to their children."

Children have an obligation to their parents to do the right thing. Parents are made in God's image, and that's what bringing children into the world is all about. Parents, do your best for your child. Mold a good person in society. As far as teachers go, they might not be respected in our society in terms of salary, but they are ones to be imparting wisdom and be listened to. Teachers show you how to do things and teach you right from wrong. For seven or eight hours a day, teachers are sort of like parents. Kids, you have to obey your teachers on things like doing your homework, because they will help make a better person out of you.

RESPECTING AUTHORITY:

I've always been taught to respect my elders and respect authority. While growing up, I did that for the most part, although—and this is the bad part of it—I learned you have to decide which of the authority figures are worthy of respect.

My parents are worthy of being respected. But if you get somebody like drug dealers, you have to learn that they are tearing away the moral fabric of society and are not worthy of being respected. They might have influence, but they don't deserve a position of authority. We've learned to respect our elders, but not all elders are worthy of being respected. A lot of people such as some televangelists use their influence to get people to wrongly follow them. Adults should know how to discern the good from the bad more readily than children do, but sometimes it doesn't work out that way.

AVOIDING DRUG AND/OR ALCOHOL ABUSE:

I tell all children to stay away from drugs. But I get tired of telling them to "Just say no," because a lot of times that's just not going to work. You have to give them a vivid picture and tell them what drugs are and what drugs do. Drugs are nothing but poison. I say, "Would you be ready to put poison into your body?" and all of them will say, "No." I say, "Well, that's the same thing that drugs do to you. It's the same deal with alcohol. Too much destroys your body and your mind." It all goes back to the family.

✳

RUSSELL MARYLAND

Dallas Cowboys defensive tackle Russell Maryland is an example of what hard work can do for an athlete.

Maryland's perseverance has paid off, and his ability to play games while hurt played a major part in the Cowboys' back-to-back Super Bowl titles in 1992 and 1993.

Maryland started twelve games in the 1993 season and was a major force behind the Cowboys' success in stopping the rush. Maryland had a hand in more than fifty tackles, including two-and-a-half sacks, six tackles behind the line of scrimmage, and twelve quarterback pressures.

Maryland's standout 1993 season mirrored his first two years in the National Football League. Taken by the Cowboys as the overall number-one pick in the 1991 draft, Maryland immediately became a key run-stopper in the Cowboys' front four. In his first season, he started the last seven games for the Cowboys and helped them make the playoffs. Maryland was voted to five different All-Rookie teams by sportswriters across the country.

A year earlier, in 1992, Maryland played most of the season with a broken toe, yet had a solid season. He made forty-nine tackles and had twelve quarterback pressures. He also recovered two fumbles, including one he returned twenty-six yards for a touchdown.

Maryland's NFL success is no surprise considering his impressive college career. Maryland was a two-time All-American at the University of Miami (Florida). In 1990, he received the Outland Trophy, awarded to the nation's top lineman. During Maryland's four years at Miami, the Hurricanes posted a 44-4 record, which included four consecutive post-season bowl victories and two national championships

Away from the field, Maryland takes an active role in community work. Among his many activities are his involvement with the Dallas inner-city Boy Scouts. He has also judged drawings as part of an anti-drug campaign in McKinney, Texas.

RUSSELL MARYLAND'S FIVE TIPS ON LIFE AND FOOTBALL:
1. In order to get respect, you have to give it.
2. It's important in any society, especially the African-American society, to strengthen the family. Strong father figures must step forward.

3. Always study ways, especially through the Bible, to be accepted unto God. From the day you're born, you're working your way to the grave. Take the right path.

4. In football, Coach Jimmy Johnson has always told us, "If you want to play football, you must have a positive mental attitude, because not everything will go your way." His formula is that positive attitude plus effort equals performance. Your athletic ability gets you only so far.

5. You've got to be a student of the game. Know what you're doing. Study your techniques. It helps to have quick feet and a sharp mind. But you've still got to be a little mean out on the field.

Author's royalties donated to Athletes in Action

T R U E
CHAMPIONS

C h a p t e r T w e n t y - t w o

KATHY GUADAGNINO

U . S . O P E N G O L F C H A M P I O N

speaks out on...

HANDLING SUCCESS:

It was in my second year on the LPGA (Ladies Professional Golf Association) tour when I ended up winning the U.S. Open. What was unique about winning at that particular time was that I went into the tournament struggling with some things, including my game, and I felt like things just weren't happening for me. I remember being back home the week before the Open and being in my room listening to the radio, when a song by Morris Chapman came on. This song had to do with how God was about to "do His greatest work in you," and for some reason—like when you read something in the Bible or hear something—it just really hit home. God had spoken to my heart, but I had no idea what it had to deal with.

Going into the Open, I experienced probably one of the toughest weeks I had ever experienced in terms of what was going on in my personal life. I was really tired. I remember being really beat going into that week. But I could sense that it was right around the corner. I remember praying to God and saying, "Lord, if anything happens

FRED VANCE

this week, it's definitely You, because I'm just pooped out." Obviously, it turned out to be an incredible week.

Another interesting thing was that two years prior to that, I had been playing in a practice round for the (1983) U.S. Open in Tulsa, Oklahoma. I was playing with a friend of mine, Barb Thomas, and I looked at her and all of a sudden I just said, "I'm going to win the U.S. Open." I was shocked, and so was she. I didn't usually say stuff like that, and it came out before I had even thought about it. Barb looked at me and said, "Was that a faith statement or what?" I didn't really think anymore of that until the week of the Open two years later.

Going into the Open week of 1985, when I was playing my practice round, it was like I could actually see myself, like I had just won the tournament. I heard what I was saying in my acceptance speech, and I was thinking, Wait a minute. I believe in dreams, but this is really weird.

Heading into the last day of the tournament, I had a one-stroke lead. On that Saturday night, all of a sudden it was like God brought back to me the thing that I had said two years earlier at that Open in Tulsa and it seemed like fate—a scary feeling actually. My next thought was, Oh Lord, don't let me mess this up. My biggest cry was just that He'd be glorified through everything. That's been my prayer since I've been out here for each week—it doesn't matter who wins; I just want God to get the glory. That's been the attitude in my heart. We went out for the final round that next day, and there was a real peace over me. Only God could give me that. It was a pretty intense situation to find myself in, and everything happened just like I had envisioned. It was really neat.

What was interesting about all this was that all of a sudden I went from being somebody who people wouldn't recognize right off, to where now I would be walking in the airport and people were saying, "Congratulations on winning the U.S. Open." Suddenly, I was catapulted into an existence where many people recognized me. That was a hard thing to deal with, because all of a sudden my privacy was being invaded. Also, I had a lot of opportunities that came my way. There were a lot of interviews and those kind of things.

I tried to keep it all in perspective. But the thing that was even more difficult to deal with in terms of success was the following year, when I wasn't living up to everybody's expectations. I had won the U.S. Open. Obviously, people thought, I should just continue on that winning streak. But I didn't. I finished out the 1985 season well, but in 1986 I didn't have a great year. All of a sudden, the media didn't want to talk to me anymore. There was other news happening. The interviews that did come my way were the ones where they asked, "Well, what's wrong with your game? Why aren't you performing like you did last year? What's wrong?"

It was a real battle for me to just remain settled within myself. I had played this game long enough to know that it has its ups and downs. It's not necessarily that something's wrong, it's just that some days you have good days, some days you have bad days, and you just learn to take it all in stride. People are always going to place expectations on you, but you just have to make sure to be settled in yourself, that you're pleasing God with your performance, and disciplining your time and priorities correctly. Knowing that, I can go out with confidence that I'm going to hit every shot the best I can and no matter what the outcome is, I know God will be pleased because I've given it my best effort.

It's not necessarily that something's wrong, it's just that some days you have good days, some days you have bad days, and you just learn to take it all in stride.

As far as dealing with success and failure, I think you really have to define what exactly success is, and what exactly failure is. If you're a Christian and giving it your all, you can never fail. From a world view, others might look at you from the standpoint of your not being on the top of the money list, but I've had moderate success out there. I'm not up there all the time, yet I feel like I have a very successful life, because God is controlling my life. He's meeting my needs, and I don't have a problem with that.

I started playing golf when I was thirteen years old. My dad got me started. I was the runner-up in the first tournament I ever entered, when I was fifteen years old. I won some other junior events, and they always seemed to be the "right" ones to win. The first big junior tournament I won was the PGA National Junior. My first college tournament victory was the NCAA (National Collegiate Athletic Association) championship, which I won as a college junior. Then came my first victory as a professional—in the U.S. Open.

When I became a Christian at age eighteen, I felt like I wanted to see if there were other things I could do. Sure, I enjoyed golf, but after becoming a Christian I had the attitude that the clubs would go into the closet and I would then go out into the mission field; go over to Africa or something.

It never worked out that way. Somewhere in there, God made it real clear to me that He had a purpose for me in golf. I had trouble putting the two together—God and golf. I wondered how His purpose could be accomplished out there. Since then, I've been able to see just how effective people in sports can be in getting the Lord's message out. They have a platform that's unique, and they also have a large audience. It's a great opportunity to be a role model as well. With it goes a lot of responsibility in portraying the right things.

I know that who and what I am is because of God. All my talents are a gift from Him, so how can I take credit for what He's given me—the abilities He's given me? I have a responsibility to use those abilities to bring Him glory. I've always been very aware of giving Him the glory for everything. During the U.S. Open I had the opportunity to go in the press room every day after my round. At the time I was so aware that it was because of God that I was in this position of winning. It wasn't my own strength. The people in the media didn't quite understand that, but that's basically what I said, and I had so many opportunities to share about that. After I had won, the fellow handling interviews said, "Kathy, if it's okay, we're going to put your name on the trophy and not God's."

When I was a new Christian, I was very vocal. As I have matured in my walk, I have used a little more wisdom in how I say things. In a couple parties that they had after the Open, I just said, "You don't have to worry about me changing. I'm still me, even though I've just won the U.S. Open." I think a lot of it had to do with my main goal in life being to please God and to honor Him with what I'm doing.

That rules out taking any credit for yourself. If you can develop a healthy attitude about who you are—who God's created you to be—it helps you from both standpoints. When dealing with failure—when everybody is not patting you on the back—you're able to pat yourself on the back, because you're God's creation. God doesn't create junk. You're pleasing to Him.

Honestly, I think a lot of times the best witness you can be is with your life. Your Christianity or your lifestyle will speak out even louder and clearer when you're dealing with adversity. It's real easy to be up and excited when you're on the top, but what really matters is when you're on the bottom and people still see you joyful and happy. That's when you can be a powerful witness. That's a hard thing to understand if you don't have that inner peace and hope. I've had bad days where I still felt happy, knowing that I had done my best and whatever score I had was just that—a score.

Golf isn't life or death, but for some of the girls on the tour it is. Golf is their life. When you see them, you can pretty much tell by the looks on their faces whether they've had a good day or a bad day. I have been told by people that they can't tell how well I'm playing from just looking at me. That's because I try to stay on an even keel. Earlier this year (1994), I was in contention at an event in Hawaii, only to finish bogey-triple bogey. What could I do? If you keep your attitude right, you can work around those things. It turned out that on the next day, I won the closest-to-the-pin contest on the eighteenth hole and the prize paid for the whole trip.

> **Honestly, I think a lot of times the best witness you can be is with your life. Your Christianity or your lifestyle will speak out even louder and clearer when you're dealing with adversity.**

BALANCING FAMILY LIFE AND A GOLF CAREER:

God has really put these things on me slowly, so I've had time to adjust. I got married in 1987. We had been married a couple years before we had our first child. That wait worked out pretty well for us, because we were both very independent, and if we had been together all the time, it would have been hard on our relationship. God brought us in slowly.

For the first couple years of marriage, I was still was having a pretty active season out on tour. I think I played about eighteen tournaments or so. Then our first daughter, Nikki, came along in 1990. What made it neat was that she was born on the Sunday morning of the 1990 U.S. Open.

Having a child took a little bit of an adjustment, especially in the first three months. Before I got married, I had become so independent taking care of all my own affairs. In marriage, God has ordained the husband as head of the household, and that for me was quite a change. I had to go through my husband and he would have final say. I remember even "getting into it" because he didn't like my driving by myself up to Orlando to get a lesson. Well, I had gone much longer distances driving by myself, and I took it as, "Well, he doesn't think I can do this," when actually he was just being protective. I finally got it through my head not to take offense with that.

For the first three months after having Nikki, I had to deal with the realization that my life was not my own anymore. My life was this little baby's life. That was very difficult.

I played a pretty full schedule the following year. Later, I was pregnant with my second daughter, Megan. With two children, it's a pretty good juggling act. Fortunately, the LPGA tour now has a day-care program. That makes it a little bit easier on us—to be able to come out and have our kids in a place where we know who's taking care of them.

The hardest thing I find now is trying to work around my schedule, because both daughters are more than two years old. I have to pay for their airline flights, so it gets very expensive if I want to travel with everybody. Sometimes, I'll go out by myself. A lot of times, if I'm going to be out for three or four weeks, my husband will come out in the middle week and bring the girls.

I don't like being away from my family for that long. It's not fair to my husband, and I don't think being separated so much is healthy for our relationship. These are things I have to consider, plus I want to be able to play well. I'm definitely a little more distracted now than I was at first, but I feel like I have my priorities in order.

✳

KATHY GUADAGNINO

Golfer Kathy Guadagnino wasted no time making her presence known on the LPGA tour.

Just two years after joining the tour in 1983, she recorded her first victory—at the prestigious U.S. Open, in 1985. Guadagnino is one of only twelve players to make the Open her first career victory.

In 1985, Guadagnino won more than $130,000 in prize money, which put her thirteenth on the LPGA's money list, her best finish going into the 1994 season.

Although Guadagnino won more than $40,000 in prize money in both 1986 and 1987, her next career victory didn't come until 1988, when she won the Konica San Jose Classic. That victory propelled Guadagnino to another stellar season, as she topped the $70,000 mark in earnings.

Since the 1988 season, Guadagnino has played sparingly on the LPGA tour. She has limited her play to fewer than twenty tournaments a year in recent years to devote time to her family, which includes daughters Nikki and Megan. Still, Guadagnino began the 1994 season closing in on the $500,000 mark in career winnings.

Guadagnino's amateur career was impressive. She was a member of the 1982 Curtis Cup and World Cup teams, and won the 1982 NCAA title while playing for the University of Tulsa.

Guadagnino's husband Joe is an associate pastor at Christian Love Fellowship Church and Dean of Student Affairs at South Florida Bible College and Theological Seminary. In addition to Bible study, Guadagnino's non-golf interests include crafts, and collecting Precious Moments and Robert Raikes Bears. She is also a "Star Trek" fan.

KATHY GUADAGNINO'S FIVE TIPS ON LIFE AND GOLF:
1. The beginning of wisdom is fear of the Lord. Proverbs is all about dealing wisely in your everyday affairs.

2. In college, I had a poster that showed a mountain goat on a trail with his head turned around, looking backward. The message said, "When God calls, don't turn around to see who's following." Following the crowd doesn't always mean you're following God.
3. The will of God will never lead you where His grace can't keep you.
4. In golf, concentrate on the basics. Keep it simple. A lot of times, we try to get too technical with the game.
5. Don't take the game too seriously. Many people live and die by their golf games, and there's so much more to life.

Author's royalties donated to Christian Love Fellowship Church

Chapter Twenty - three

ANDRE CASON
WORLD CHAMPION SPRINTER
speaks out on...

**OVERCOMING STEREOTYPES
AND ADVERSITY:**

The first thing I had to overcome was my perceived height disadvantage. I am only five-foot-seven, and I think the shortest sprinter I've ever beaten is about five-foot-nine. I have also been doubted many, many times by people who think of me as being only an indoor sprinter. Without trying to sound cute, I think it's safe to say that many people have sold me short. But that's okay.

During the competitive year of 1992, I was just about to overcome that stereotype of being too short. I really believe I was on the verge of emerging as the best sprinter in the world—indoor or outdoor—that year, when I hurt myself. That was at the Olympic Trials in Modesto, California. In the first thirty meters of a first-round heat, I tore up an Achilles' tendon, which ruined the year competitively for me. As for adversity, I would have to say that the Achilles' injury is the biggest obstacle that I've ever had to cross—up to this point.

Getting back to my stature, people have been saying that I'm too short to be a really good outdoor sprinter ever since I was in high school. But I compensate for my lack of height with my strength. I think it's safe to say that pound for pound I am the strongest sprinter in the world. I've had to make up for my "shortcomings" with improved strength, and that's how I've gotten ahead as a sprinter. Of course, there's also my faith in God.

I wouldn't say that people have picked on me because of my size, but I know that I've been underestimated many times. It's true that most people are underestimated for one reason or another. That's where determination on the part of the individual comes in. As far as myself, all that matters is that I have faith in myself and I have faith in God. That's why I've been able to achieve everything I have achieved so far.

People have been saying that I'm too short to be a really good outdoor sprinter ever since I was in high school. But I compensate for my lack of height with my strength.

I was brought up by my grandmother as well as by my mother, and that's where the basis for my faith comes from. Let me put it to you this way: With the upbringing I had, I was afraid to stray away from God. Likewise, I had faith in the talents He had given me. While in high school, I was also a good football and baseball player, so I always felt that there would be something I could excel at, regardless of my size or what other expectations people had of me.

One thing my grandmother instilled in me was a desire to be the best I could be no matter what I did and not to think of my height as a disadvantage, but as an advantage. She also said that my height disadvantage would not be an excuse for me, either. What she said really helped me out and helped put things in perspective for me.

Keeping things in perspective was important for me after I got injured in the 1992 Olympic Trials. Although I really believe that if I hadn't gotten injured I would be the world champion today, I know that things happen for a reason, whether they be good or bad. You might not know at that particular time, but God will reveal it to you in His good time.

Sometimes people in the type of injury situation I was in will say, "Why me, why me?" Even I found myself saying that, and that's when I was started realizing things I hadn't understood before. For one thing, my injury, and having to miss the next few months while recovering, showed me which people around me were really loyal to me and which weren't. It wasn't long until I figured out that people who were supposedly supporting me weren't genuine at all.

To this day, I really believe that if I hadn't had that injury—resulting in many of those people who said they were loyal to me actually leaving me—I might have ended up being led astray from the right path. All things considered, everything that happened to me happened for the best, although I didn't really realize it at the time.

I also want to teach my children that it's okay to be successful. Sometimes you will get sidetracked, but do not be worried about failure.

Somewhere in all this, it became evident to me that money is the root of all evil. In fact, money and greed are the two most evil things on the face of this earth. I don't really concern myself with money. I have other priorities in life. I will say that I hope to provide enough money for my children so that they will be able to go to any major university they want to go to without having to rely on getting a scholarship. Or if they decide at age eighteen not to go to college, I want them to still have that money to do something like open up their own business or something else constructive like that.

I also want to teach my children that it's okay to be successful. Sometimes you will get sidetracked, but do not be worried about failure. Earning money for those things is a good thing to strive for, but other than that I run just for the pure aspect of competition and the pleasure it brings me.

My life had been pretty stable for me up until the time I was injured. After getting hurt, I ended up in a cast from my toes to my hip for a long time. The injury and how it happened didn't destroy me mentally, because I am a very strong-willed person. The key to what got me through the injury was my fiancée—who is now my wife—my father, and my grandmother. They were with me every single day when I was recovering and I'll never forget that. But first and foremost, there was my faith in God. I always had faith in God that He would see me through this, and I depended on Him to get me through it. My ultimate faith was in God.

Right after I was injured there were people telling me that this was only a test. I had to overcome that adversity, and the way I did overcome that adversity was through renewing my faith in God. To the everyday person who might not be a believer, I could probably explain all of this, but it would take an awful lot of thinking on their part. But I think I could explain my faith very well to people who are familiar with the world of track and field. Anyone who knows anything about track knows that you don't suffer a career-threatening injury one year and then come back the next year to win a silver medal at the World Championships, like I did. I certainly couldn't have done that on my own, without God. That in itself is testimony to my faith in the Lord and what He's done in bringing me through all this. I really believe that.

I guess you could say that I show my faith through the examples of how well I've done in my running. See, if I were to go out to elementary schools, junior highs, and high schools—like I do now—and just tell everyday people about what the Lord has done for me—without my referring to track and field—they would probably think I am crazy. But God has put me on this earth and given me the ability, and He is using my ability to show other people, especially young people, who He is and what He can do. Older people who are nonbelievers still might not understand, because they probably are too set in their ways to believe in what I would have to say.

If I can say just one thing, whether it be just a sentence or a phrase, if I can touch just one person with my message, they will tell a friend and on and on it goes. However, I don't necessarily liken myself to being a role model. I have two young children myself, and I just want to be a role model to them; that's my first responsibility—my family. However, again, we as professional athletes have to take some responsibility in terms of being a role model, and I do accept that. My dad has told me that since day one. You have to take that responsibility, because you're being seen on television; you're being seen in the newspapers; and you're being heard about in many places. Like it or not, you have that responsibility.

When I was injured, I was actually out for about six months rehabilitating, although it was seven to eight months before I could again compete. That's how serious an injury I had. When I finally got out of my cast, I could hardly walk. There had been a lot of atrophy in my leg and there was still a lot of soreness in my Achilles'; it was still tender. I had to go to rehabilitation every day for three hours, sometimes even six hours a day. I had to do a lot of stuff in the swimming pool, and on various machines. Needless to say, it was very painful.

The part of my body that was really damaged the most of all was my head. Like I said earlier, it didn't destroy me mentally, but it played some tricks on me. Before my injury, I had been so enthused about running in the Olympics because I had no doubt that I was going to be the Olympic champion. That sounds arrogant, but it is something I really believed in. That's just how strong I felt about myself and my abilities to succeed. I knew it was just a matter of time. Then for something to happen so suddenly shook me. For a while, I was really down; I was really damaged.

It was a really deep, deep valley in my life. But somewhere in all that, I was saying to myself and trying to believe that "I'm not going to let this get the best of me." I kept repeating that over and over, knowing I would eventually start believing it. The tough part of my injury was that I went down in the first thirty meters of that race. That memory kept coming back to me as a sort of psychological barrier over the first fifty meters of races. I had to overcome the fear of reinjuring myself the same way in the early part of a race. In fact, I was actually terrified in the early part of the races. While I didn't feel any pain, my mind kept telling me that something might happen at any moment.

Going into 1994, I was feeling stronger than I've ever been, even stronger than I was during my successful year in 1993. This isn't something that I brag about, though, because I don't want people to hear me say it and then twist it around to sound like I'm being big-headed or whatever. I just know where I've come from and I know what I feel and I feel really good about the recovery that I have made. Still, I don't want to come across as egotistical, because I know that another thing my dad told me a long time ago is that, "You don't want to be going around and telling everybody how good you are, running your mouth off!" What he was saying was that whatever I had to show shouldn't be coming out of my mouth, but should be displayed on the track.

The injury experience in 1992 was something that humbled me a lot. Another thing that I learned from that whole experience is that people disappear as quickly as they come in. I also learned that all that glitters is not gold.

The injury experience in 1992 was something that humbled me a lot. Another thing that I learned from that whole experience is that people disappear as quickly as they come in. I also learned that all that glitters is not gold. Since 1992, I've gotten a new coach—Loren Seagraves—and he's really been a godsend for me. I say that because I had met Loren a long time before that and had then told him that someday he would be my coach. I don't know what brought me to say that, but I really believed it and that's exactly how it worked out.

It just shows me that there's someone else who has His hand on my life. There's no other way that I can explain what has happened. Again, it was God speaking to me. I feel now that I have a story to tell, a good testimony, because of the adversity I've been through. I am a golden child, and I say that because I know that my career could very easily have ended with that injury in 1992.

I think I put things in perspective a lot more now, because I know you can't go out there as a track athlete and really expect to win every single time. That would be like a boxer going out there expecting he's never going to get hit. You're going to get hit sometime. It's like in track—you might win, but there are going to be times when you're going to get hit, too. You have to be able to deal with that as well as deal with the victories.

To be successful, it takes more than just telling yourself that you're going to be successful. I know when I'm ready and I know when I'm not ready, and I can tell you when I'm focused and when

I'm not. I'll be honest about it and not try to fool myself or anybody else into thinking anything different.

ANDRE CASON

Sprinter Andre Cason has always been a record setter in track.

From high school to college to the World Championships, Cason has made a name for himself with his fast times. Cason, who competes in both indoor and outdoor events, is now recognized as one of the world's top sprinters.

And Cason's past successes show that he deserves it.

In the 1993 season, Cason was the United States National Champion in the 100-meter dash. He also was the silver medalist in the 100-meter race at the World Championships, where he also won a gold medal as part of the victorious 4 X 100-meter relay team.

Cason, who missed much of the 1992 season with a serious Achilles' tendon injury, came back stronger than ever in 1993. Case in point: At the U.S. outdoor championships, he won the 100-meter event in the second-fastest time ever—9.79 seconds, just .01 behind the world record (as of 1993).

Cason also had much success prior to 1993. He is a two-time and current world-record holder in the sixty-meter indoor dash, and was ranked No. 1 by *Track and Field News* in 1992. Later that year, he was named the World Men's Indoor Athlete of the Year. Cason also was a gold medalist in the 1990 Goodwill Games.

Cason's college career at Texas A&M University was equally impressive. He was a two-time NCAA All-American and was a member of the NCAA champion 4 X 100-meter relay team in 1989. Cason was also named the 1989 World University Games Most Outstanding Performer after setting meet records in the 100-meter dash and as part of the 4 X 100-meter relay team.

ANDRE CASON'S FIVE TIPS ON LIFE AND TRACK:

1. Learn how to pray. Anyone can pray and ask, but knowing what you're praying for, why you're praying, and whom you're praying to is what's important. There's a difference between praying and asking.
2. Never stray away from God.
3. Listen to your spouse, because there are times when you think that you know it all and your spouse will see something that you don't see, but should see.
4. In track, only you know if you're really hurt. Listen to your body and trust in how you know you feel.
5. If you don't believe in yourself, no one else will.

Author's royalties donated to Fellowship of Christian Athletes

C h a p t e r   T w e n t y - f o u r

EDDIE HILL
TOP FUEL DRAGSTER CHAMPION
speaks out on...

PAYING YOUR DUES:

It has been a long road and there have been many disappointments and a lot of dues to be paid along the way. Our team never gave up hope, and we finally grabbed the brass ring when we won the world championship in 1993, which allowed us to obtain more financial sponsorship. In a way, sponsorship is more important than the championship, because financial assistance provides us with tools to win other championships if we do things right.

We had several good reasons to give up and quit, if we had been so inclined. The easiest alternative would have been to stay retired back in the mid-sixties after I experienced a bad engine fire at Green Valley Raceway near Fort Worth. Smoke from burning fuel and oil blocked my vision until I got the car stopped with the left front wheel just off the left-hand side of the drag strip. If I had obeyed my natural inclination to pull the car back to the left, I would have crashed into trees and we wouldn't be having this conversation (used as the basis for this chapter).

I had always thought that if the car scared me, I wouldn't climb into it again. Well, the fire shook me up enough that I didn't go to the next race I had planned to attend in West Texas, and I didn't race cars anymore for a long, long time.

My first high-speed, drag-boat crash came in 1979, and was caused by a supercharger explosion so severe that it spun the boat around backward. I have a photo that was taken as the boat threw me out in front of it and my body tripped the finish-line timing lights at 166 miles per hour. I didn't have my personal parachute hooked up as I normally would have, and I skipped like a stone across the water nine times before stopping a quarter of a mile from where I was ejected from the boat. I was not injured, other than my whole body being one huge bruise.

I was involved in another high-speed crash in 1984 while racing my blown fuel hydroplane. The boat was traveling more than 217 miles per hour, when it crashed just past the finish line. I ended up with seven broken bones, a concussion, puncture wounds in my face and leg, and nearly lost my eyes. That could have been another reason to end my career.

Instead of quitting altogether, a few months after the crash, when I was sufficiently healed and could drive again, my wife Ercie and I switched back to asphalt racing, which we perceive to be the safest form of motor sports. We wanted to do it badly enough to cash in my retirement-income policies that I had worked for all my life. We also sold our new Corvette, which was the only new Corvette I had ever owned. We raced on our own bucks with no sponsorship until our money ran out about a year later in 1986. As it turned out, we hadn't actually squandered our life savings, but it seemed so at the time, since the car wasn't running well enough to qualify at most races. We hadn't learned our way around yet—hadn't learned the ropes. We weren't racing well enough to secure a sponsor.

Then we met a complete stranger at the Texas Motorplex in Ennis, Texas, by the name of Bill Bishop. Out of Christian love, he walked up to us and said, "You look like you could use some help. I'll help you." He stepped in and became our benefactor. He said he would try to keep us racing until corporate sponsorship came along, and that's exactly what he did. Bill bankrolled us and kept our team alive financially until we secured sponsorship help at the end of the 1987 season.

Until Bill Bishop stepped in in 1986, we were basically out of money and out of parts, and didn't have any way to go on. My spirit didn't want to quit. I wanted to continue to race, but I had no money for parts. You can't race a car without pistons. Bill donated hundreds of thousands of dollars to our racing effort without asking for anything in return. He had nothing to gain, except the satisfaction of helping us.

By the end of 1987, we were lucky enough to be running fairly well and had set a national speed record. While we were at the World Finals in Pomona, California (the last race of the year), my Big Boss upstairs woke me up at 3:00 A.M., and I had what remains my only two-way conversation with Him. He asked me in no uncertain terms if I was ready for The Big Time. He really got my attention. I woke up in a cold sweat with what felt like electricity on my skin. It was a very strange feeling. I had a clear impression that my Big Boss was talking to me, and I had never had that happen before. I wasn't a young man at that time, either.

My spirit didn't want to quit. I wanted to continue to race, but I had no money for parts. You can't race a car without pistons.

It was an impressive event for me, and I wanted to be sure that I gave Him the right response, but I didn't have an immediate answer. I stopped to think about what He really meant. The way I interpreted His question was whether I could handle myself properly and be a public representative with the right kind of values, should I be lucky enough to get a sponsor and be able to race the way I wanted. Perhaps youngsters or someone else would look up to me as a role model. That would be my chance to contribute something, like sending out a positive message that you don't have to lie, cheat, steal, take drugs, or live an immoral life to be successful.

After I sorted it out in my mind, I realize that maybe drag racing wasn't quite as frivolous as I had thought. That might sound strange coming from someone who has devoted his life to it, but I thought that maybe racing wasn't all that important in the great scheme of things. In this particular introspection, I understood that racing done the right way wasn't important in terms of elapsed time and speed, but is the effort and dedication that it takes to make a race car run that gets the attention of people and can influence them in a positive way. When I looked at it from that perspective, all of a sudden drag racing was important, if I did it right. So my answer to God was, "Yes, I'm ready."

That might sound strange coming from someone who has devoted his life to it, but I thought that maybe racing wasn't all that important in the great scheme of things.

Within what seemed like hours, but was probably a few days, I was approached by not only Super Shops, but also Pennzoil. They asked if they could sponsor our car. Prior to my conversation with the Big Boss, we had shot-gunned proposals over what seemed like the whole world looking for sponsorship, but to no avail. When I was asked one question by Him and what apparently was the proper answer, the sponsorship happened almost instantly. It happened so quickly, it's still difficult to believe.

Talk about favor among men! During the entire 1988 season, so many blessings came our way. We were fortunate enough to run the first four-second elapsed time in history, win seven national events, set national elapsed time and speed records, win *Car Craft Magazine*'s Person of the Year award, and we had a fantastic year overall.

Again, all of it kicked in immediately after that conversation. The nuts and bolts we were using were still the same. The knowledge I had about drag racing was the same. We had the same crew. What was different was our commitment to proper values and being proper role models, should anybody choose to pattern his or her life after us. We wanted to be sure that anyone looking at us thought we were a force for good, not evil.

I had one of the most famous crashes in drag racing history at the first race of the 1989 season. My top fuel dragster blew over backward at 270 miles per hour, flew vertically through the finish timing lights thirty feet off the ground, and came to rest approximately an eighth of a mile from where it had become airborne. The crash totally destroyed the car, except for my little roll cage. I think the good Lord had me in His hands that time. He probably bruised His knuckles on that one, and I came out of it with only bruised knees.

When I stepped out of the car, my first thought was that I had just destroyed the world's quickest and fastest race car. Immediately after that, I said to myself, "Wait a minute, turkey, you just lived through what had to be one of the all-time worst crashes in the world and you're totally unhurt. You need to thank The Man and get your priorities straight." I did thank the Lord and have continued to thank Him daily since then.

On the day of that crash, Darrell Gwynn came over and offered us his spare chassis to use for the remainder of the race. It was a selfless act on Darrell's part, a beautiful testimonial in itself. Darrell didn't say, "We're praying for you, Eddie," and then walk away. Instead, he said, "I'll loan you my spare car at no charge." It was a very Christian thing to do, and uncommon in many forms of motor sports.

We borrowed Darrell's bare chassis and put our engine, rear end, computer, wheels, tires, and clutch into it. Twenty-four hours later, it was a race car and we qualified it into the race. That was quite an accomplishment. It would have been easier to go home and regroup after the crash, but our team put forth the effort necessary to get back into the race. We didn't want to quit.

Ercie, our team, and I believe it's important to project a wholesome family image. We like to treat people the way we would like to be treated. Do unto others. We try not to just say that, but to live it out by example. We try to project an image not of Bible-thumping, religious zealots, but of people who are happy, and never at the expense of others.

We try not to take without giving. We try to interact with our fans and give them the autographs and attention they desire, and to meet their needs as we talk to them as equals. The fact that our fans are on the other side of the pit area ropes doesn't mean they are worth any less as human beings than we are. We try to let them know that, and seem to have pretty good luck with it.

When we have a chance to speak to youth groups, we try to tell them that we all have the same basic equipment to work with. Success might not come easily, and there might be many dues to pay; but it will ultimately come to those who want it badly enough, handle themselves properly, and try hard enough to achieve it.

❋

EDDIE HILL

Eddie Hill just keeps on going and going on the drag-racing circuit. He has been involved in motor sports racing for more than forty years and continued to set drag racing records at age fifty-seven during the 1993 National Hot Rod Association (NHRA) season. Hill won the NHRA top fuel championship and won six NHRA national events along the way, tying the record for most victories in a single NHRA season. Each time he won an NHRA national event, Hill set a new record for the oldest driver to do so.

Hill achieved all of these goals in his "comeback." After a stellar drag racing career in the 1950s and 1960s, he retired in 1966 following the aforementioned fire in his race car. For those early achievements, Hill was inducted into the NHRA Division IV Hall of Fame in 1978.

After racing motorcycles professionally for eight years (from 1966 to 1974), Hill raced drag boats for ten years (1974-84) and held all four drag boat nationally sanctioned speed records simultaneously. He won literally every honor and championship in drag boat racing at least once. When Hill returned to top fuel drag racing in 1985, he soon began to set land speed records, his first in 1987 at 287 miles per hour.

Hill enjoys spending time with his wife and team manager, Ercie, his son Dustin and daughter Sabrina. He likes to listen to classical music and opera, and enjoys eating M&Ms.